KT-403-749

A Pocket Book on
Microwave Cooking

Hints and recipes

Cecilia Norman

Octopus Books

Contents

First published 1985 by
Octopus Books Limited
59 Grosvenor Street
London W1

Reprinted 1986

© 1985 Octopus Books Limited

ISBN 0 7064 2313 5

Produced by Mandarin Publishers Ltd
22a Westlands Road, Quarry Bay,
Hong Kong

Introduction

THE ADVANTAGES OF A MICROWAVE OVEN

In cooking matters great grandmother had no choice. Her kitchen equipment was minimal; washing machines were non-existent, dishwashers unheard of, and non-stick saucepans not invented. A microwave oven was as improbable as a space flight. She had to do everything the long and laborious way but she did have plenty of time.

All this has changed. No-one seems to have time to spare, men as well as women do the cooking, and many children get their own tea. But we are lucky because we do have modern appliances to help us, and the microwave oven is the most revolutionary of them all. It is a wonderful cooking device which carries out four main processes – thawing, cooking, short cuts and reheating – with speed, ease and safety. It is portable so that you can move it from room to room or from house to house and it can be carried by one strong or two weak people. It doesn't need any special installation so you don't need to have an electrician in: domestic models work off an ordinary plug.

The microwave oven is ideal for small kitchens because it doesn't create additional heat, it keeps the smells in and fits comfortably on to a work surface or sturdy table. It is easy to keep clean as there can be no burnt-on grease. A rub over with a cloth moistened with washing-up liquid is sufficient to clean it. One of the boons of the microwave oven is that it reduces clearing-up to a minimum because the cooking is done in the serving dishes, if they are suitable, or on your plates.

USING A MICROWAVE OVEN

The microwave oven can take the place of a conventional oven and a hob for most cooking processes but it cannot replace the grill unless this is built-in or there is a browning device. Unlike the conventional oven the microwave has no dry heat so that it is unable to produce food with a crisp crust outside and a soft interior. But foods which are normally served moist produce, in many instances, superior results to those obtained from cooking conventionally. For example, all fillets of fish remain in a more moist and therefore more delicious condition.

Because of the speed of cooking, precious vitamins are retained. Since far less water is used in microwave cookery, any mineral salts and flavours that come out of the food help to produce a very tasty liquor. If you are going to drain the food, save this liquor for use in sauces. Fish liquor can be added to parsley sauce for instance.

No deep frying

Apart from grilling, the only process that the microwave oven is not able to carry out is deep frying. This is because there is no temperature control and the hot fat could overheat and catch fire. As with conventional cooking, much depends upon the quality of the food and the talents of the cook. It takes a little practice to become accustomed to the different techniques involved, but these are not difficult to master.

Use your microwave oven for what it does best and include in this all the ancillary tasks that it can carry out so easily when used in conjunction with conventional cooking (e.g. to soften butter). At home I select menus that I know will be successful when cooked by microwave.

Store of goodies

When I have plenty of time to spare I roast potatoes, make Yorkshire pudding, éclairs and tender casseroles in my conventional oven. I then store them in the freezer knowing that my microwave oven will be able to thaw and reheat them perfectly. It is indispensable, undemanding, requiring only a wipe over with a damp cloth.

Hot and cold spots

Regardless of the type and model of your oven there will inevitably be certain parts which receive more microwave energy than others. Turntables and convection systems have been added to recent models of microwave ovens to combat the irregular distribution of temperature.

Whichever model you choose, remember that, with familiarity, you will soon recognise any hot and cold spots which exist in your oven.

Wave effect tests

A simple test to find out which parts of your oven are 'hot' and which parts are 'cold' or 'cooler' is to put as large a container as will fit on the microwave oven shelf and half fill it with cold water. Put the oven on high and watch the water; the hotter parts of your oven are those where the water bubbles first. The more accurate way to test this is to spread out nine containers made of a similar material on the oven shelf. Partly fill them with equal quantities of cold water, switch on at full power and observe which bubbles first. Whichever method you use do not boil the water for too long as it tends to explode during prolonged boiling (air becomes trapped in the bubbles which in turn causes spattering).

Thawing techniques

One of the main uses of the microwave is thawing. This can mean straightforward defrosting when no further cooking is required, for example frozen raspberries or blackberries may be served raw with just a little cream. It is ideal for thawing convenience foods or conventionally cooked dishes stored in the freezer which may require further reheating or prime cooking.

Food that cannot be stirred

Due to the idiosyncrasies of the microwave oven, parts of the food may thaw more quickly than others, and this particularly applies to foods which cannot be stirred. The two things to remember are that the microwave oven has hot areas and cold areas, and these do not change, and secondly that microwaves cook in a circle so that the middle receives less microwave energy.

Stirrable food

Generally speaking liquids and stirrable foods can be thawed at full power but any food that cannot be re-arranged, such as a pie or pudding, should be thawed on low. If your oven has variable control but no indicated defrost setting, use about one-third of full power, or one-third around the dial.

Thawing only

To thaw stirrable items that are to be served cold without further cooking, either defrost on low, stirring occasionally, or on full power stirring frequently and, after stirring, test. If any parts feel warmer to the touch than others it is best to leave the dish to stand for a few minutes, then test again before additional defrosting.

Meat can be thawed and on the plate in minutes.

Don't overthaw
It is never a good idea to overthaw as overthawing signifies the beginning of cooking and great care should be taken with bakery items which will go stale more quickly if they are overthawed. All fresh protein foods requiring subsequent cooking must be thoroughly defrosted before proceeding. Fish, meat and poultry come into this category and the signs of incomplete thawing are visually discernible. Some ovens can be programmed to carry out these processes consecutively but I think that it is always wise to test that the food is completely thawed before proceeding. Should you notice the tell-tale opaque colour round the edges of the food while the middle is still raw, shield these parts carefully with foil, which, of course, must not touch the sides of the oven, and continue microwaving. A small amount of overthawing will not affect the finished food except in the case of steaks.

All food in a minimal amount of liquid responds better when it is thawed uncovered. Foods with a high liquid content such as soups or stews will thaw more quickly if they are three-quarters covered. As soon as the thawing takes place round the edges, begin to stir from time to time and break up the lumps when the mixture is soft.

Speeded-up process
To speed up the defrosting of the middle portions, make a well in the centre and stand an empty cup in it (ensure that the cup is suitable for microwave ovens). If the solids and liquid have separated during freezing it is best to thaw ice-side up. Ice is very slow to thaw and most of the microwaves pass through it. As the trapped food heats, it melts the ice. If the ice side were underneath, the pieces of food might overcook before the liquid thawed.

Thawing and reheating

When a cooked item is to be thawed and then reheated, use a narrow dish deep enough to allow for the fact that when thawed the food may overflow. As defrosting continues, gravies and sauces tend to seep and dry up around the edges before the central mass has thawed out.

Dishes which cannot be stirred must be turned during

the defrosting period. If your oven has no low or defrost control, you can thaw at full power by giving short bursts of microwave energy followed by a lengthy rest period. For example, for poultry allow one minute each 500 g (1 lb) of food weight on high, followed by a ten-minute standing period. Reposition or turn over, then repeat as necessary. Frozen vegetables such as peas, beans and carrots need no thawing prior to cooking but the cooking process may take a little longer. Individual thawing techniques are included in the A-Z section from page 26.

Cooking techniques

Once you understand your own oven you should not have any difficulty in achieving high cooking standards. Many of the cooking techniques are similar to those required for thawing.

Turning

In some recipes you are instructed to turn the food. This may be described as rotating, and it means giving the dish a quarter- or half-turn, or turning the dish through 90° or 180°. This should never be confused with turning the food itself over.

The reason for turning the dishes is to ensure that the food passes equally through all the hot and cold spots. Where your oven is fitted with a turntable this may not always be necessary, but the turntable cooks in a bull's-eye design, so that food that is centrally placed may not cook absolutely evenly unless the dish is repositioned. Small individual dishes (such as ramekins) being cooked simultaneously should each be given a 180° turn regardless of the design of the oven shelf and they should not be placed in the central area.

Repositioning

When cooking a number of large items in a shallow dish, you should move each from the sides to the middle at least once during cooking. When large pieces are cooked in a deep container, they should be repositioned or stirred. Microwaves cannot penetrate uniformly to a depth of more than 4 cm (1½ in) and in many cases it is far less than this.

Large thick items, such as a large jacket potato, should be turned over half-way during cooking. A very large piece of food such as a chicken should be turned over four times so that each side is equally cooked. The pieces nearest to the top of the oven will cook most quickly. All turning, stirring and repositioning should be equally divided throughout the planned cooking time.

Stirring

This is a very important factor in microwave cookery. Recipe instructions which state 'frequently' mean that certain foods such as custards and others which might curdle should be stirred every 15 seconds. Less delicate foods such as meat, poultry and vegetables should be stirred every two or three minutes. 'Stirring occasionally' indicates stirring three or four times during the cooking period. You can compare 'stir frequently' in microwave cookery with 'stir continuously' in conventional cooking. In conventional cooking this prevents burning or congealing on the bottom of the pan. In microwave cookery it prevents overcooking round the edges. 'Stirring occasionally' or 'from time to time' means the same thing.

In microwave cookery it is unwise to leave any spoons in the food during cooking: metal implements would cause damage to the magnetron and the oven, and wooden spoons become hot.

Covering

Cover all foods which have to be kept moist or those which will benefit from cooking in steam. These dishes also need stirring during cooking. Use either a lid made of suitable material with an aperture to allow the steam to escape, or three-quarters cover the dish with cling film (see page 24). Some foods benefit from being lightly covered with grease-proof (wax) paper. This encourages speedy cooking without causing the food to become too soggy. Never cover with foil as this would prevent the food from cooking at all.

Popping

Some foods pop and spit – e.g. fish with bones and poultry (because of sinews) and these should be covered during cooking to prevent spattering on the oven ceiling and walls.

After cooking this type of food do not remove the covering immediately, but allow extra standing time. The hot food could erupt in your face. Always remove the cover from the side furthest away from you.

To cook vegetables to perfection, three-quarters cover with cling film and stir every 2 to 3 minutes.

All foods enclosed in skin, peel or shell will burst unless they are pricked, scored or cut. Included in this are tomatoes, apples, livers, kidneys and eggs. Never cook an egg in the shell in the microwave oven.

Standing times

The intense heat built up in the food during cooking causes cooking to continue after the microwave oven is switched off. Allow a rest or standing time before serving so that the heat can equalize. Some foods can be eaten almost immediately and these include fillets of fish, and small or cut-up vegetables. Larger items such as a jacket potato would be too hot to eat if served immediately. If time is allowed for the heat to equalize, you won't be so likely to burn your mouth.

Because of this intense build-up of heat, it is a good idea, particularly with large joints of meat and jacket potatoes, to take them out of the oven before cooking has completely finished and then tent them with foil (see page 24). This has the dual advantage of maintaining the heat before serving and at the same time saves fuel by cutting down on cooking time.

Timing

Whether cooking by microwave or conventional means, timing is an important factor. Because microwave cooking is so much quicker overall, the cooking time will be shorter. A few foods are cooked spectacularly fast in the microwave oven – potatoes in their jackets, baked apples, beetroot and cakes. But as a rule microwave cooking is between one-fifth and one-quarter of the traditional.

Timings given in microwave cookery books cannot be precise because so much depends on the starting temperature of the food, the quantity, the shape and the density. For instance dishes cooked simultaneously take longer than individual items; one jacket potato cooks more quickly than three. Individual microwave ovens also vary in their microwave output and sometimes the internal dimensions have an effect. Since these timing instructions can only be a guide, until you are accustomed to microwave cookery and conversant with your own appliance, always cook for less than the time given. It is always possible to cook a little more but nothing can remedy over-cooking.

Cooking terms

In microwave cookery, descriptive words such as high, medium, low or full power, half power and one-third power are used. Conventional cookery terms include boiling, simmering or poaching, cooking over fierce heat or gentle cooking. As a rule of thumb, when conventional instructions indicate high temperatures, use high or full power microwave energy. Similarly, gentle cooking means cooking on low. The timing on items requiring short cooking periods is far more critical than longer-cooked foods. For example, scrambled egg may take one and a half minutes to cook but it would be spoilt if given two minutes; a large piece of meat, however, will suffer little if overcooked by three to four minutes. 'Stirring frequently', 'stirring occasionally' or perhaps 'stirring once' during cooking, should also be related to the anticipated length of cooking. It is better to judge the cooking stages by testing with a fork or by keeping a constant watch on the food, rather than adhering strictly to cooking times.

Speed

Timing should not be confused with speed. Timing always means number of minutes and seconds but speed can also mean a variation of power levels. Compare this to the speeds on a bicycle or gears in a car.

Varying speeds, cooking levels and power settings are sometimes described in different words on different makes of ovens. Generally, the maximum amount of power a microwave oven can supply is 700 watts and this can be controlled to varying degrees. Some microwave ovens have two power settings: usually full (100% power) and low or defrost (30-40% power). Others have more descriptive control settings, employing terms such as 'defrost', 'simmer', 'roast' and 'full power'. On more sophisticated microwave ovens the power can be controlled more precisely and may be varied on a scale from 1 to 10. With variable power control, foods requiring very gentle cooking can be cooked to perfection. The table on page 14 shows how the three power levels used in this book (low, medium and full) may correspond to the settings on your microwave oven. Therefore if your microwave oven has variable power the corresponding settings may be seen at a glance.

COMPARATIVE CONTROL SETTINGS

	Low			Medium			Full			
0	10	20	30	40	50	60	70	80	90	100%
										COOK
									HIGH POWER	
									FULL POWER	
									FULL POWER	
									FULL POWER	
								HIGH		
							ROAST			
						ROAST				
					MEDIUM					
			LOW AND DEFROST							
			DEFROST							
				SIMMER						
					SIMMER					
		DEFROST								
	LOW	DEFROST								
			DEFROST							
WARM										
0	1	2	3	4	5	6	7	8	9	10

Power settings used in this book compared with those used on popular microwave ovens.

Reheating

When food is reheated by microwave it is neither dried up nor too soft and soggy. When reheating or keeping food hot in a conventional oven or steamer the original texture can be somewhat affected. The microwave oven reheats perfectly. When preparing dishes for the freezer, slight undercooking is a must, so that during reheating there will be no possibility of overcooking.

The reheating technique depends upon the type of dish. Any food in a sauce or gravy should be loosely covered. Dry foods intended to be served crisp may be reheated without a cover or, for speedier results, covered with a sheet of paper kitchen towel. The paper towel will also protect the oven lining should any food pop or spatter. Some ovens have a particularly energetic fan which may blow this paper off so secure it with a wooden cocktail stick pressed into the food. Gravied and sauced foods are best reheated

Stacking rings are available from microware suppliers.

in a narrow deep dish rather than a wide shallow one so that the gravy will not dry up round the edges of the dish. Food that can be stirred or repositioned will reheat more evenly. Servings which are to be left undisturbed to retain their attractive appearance must be turned through 90° at four equal intervals during the anticipated reheating times.

Dishes containing a single cooked ingredient heat more easily than a combination of foods on a plate which are likely to be of different densities and sizes. When cooked dishes have been frozen, reheating can proceed immediately after the food has thawed. To speed the process, transfer the frozen foods to the refrigerator a few hours in advance. From normal refrigerator temperature, meat and poultry, casseroles and stews require approximately two minutes each 300 ml (½ pint) to reheat. To achieve an even temperature stir during reheating (see page 10).

Soup

An individual bowl of soup reheats in two to three minutes depending on the ingredients; thick vegetable soup will take longer than a consommé. You will see the soup boiling round the edges after about one and a half minutes but this is no indication that it has reached serving temperature, the centre may still be cool. Stir as soon as bubbling occurs and then microwave a little longer. This ensures that the liquid is uniformly hot.

Fast and slow foods

Fruit and vegetables will reheat more quickly if they are three-quarters covered. Fruits with a high sugar content take about 30 seconds to heat and most vegetables take about 45 seconds for the average single serving. The exceptions are potatoes and pasta. Although they take more time to cook in the first place, they retain their heat longer, when fully reheated, so if they are cooked first and taken out while the quicker-cooking foods are being reheated they will not cool down too much.

Plated meals

When arranging foods on a plate for reheating, arrange the thick or dense items towards the outside and the smaller thinner pieces in the centre. Non-metallic stacking rings are ideal if two or three plates are to be reheated at the same time; you only need to cover the top one (see picture on page 15). Plastic lids, which can be used to cover plates and then stacked, are also available. Stagger the foodstuffs so that a particular variety is not vertically above itself. Potatoes are particularly slow to reheat so it might be advisable to arrange them in two places around the edge of the plate. You can usually feel when all the food is hot by placing your hand underneath the plate. Peas are best reheated in a small pile stirring them first to provide some gaps between them.

Never try to reheat two plates or more sitting directly one on top of the other, even though they may be covered with plastic cling film. Reheating is slower when the passage of air is restricted. As a rule no more than three plates can be reheated at any one time. An average meal on a plate will take two and a half to three and a half minutes to reheat from cold.

Reheating times

A double quantity of food does not necessarily take twice the time. Allow time and three-quarters for two plates or two quantities, and two and a quarter times for three quantities. Reheat on full power or three-quarters power unless the ingredients are delicate, for example egg custards. Spaghetti in a sauce is best reheated when the sauce and spaghetti are stirred together first. Otherwise place the spaghetti round the outside and the sauce in the centre of the plate.

Take extreme care when serving reheated puddings containing syrup or jam. Doughnuts remain almost cold outside yet the jam inside becomes burning hot. The same applies to syrup or jam sponge puddings.

No more left-overs

If you have a refrigerator you can pre-cook a variety of dishes, providing each member of the family with a menu to suit each individual taste at that particular meal. There need be no waste since only the portions required are reheated. Reheated foods should no longer be described as left-overs for they are a definite bonus of well-planned microwave cooking.

Containers

You can use most of your bowls, dishes and casseroles when cooking by microwave though there are a few exceptions. Because the microwaves need to reach the food to 'cook' it, they must pass freely through the container. Some materials and shapes are more efficient than others but a much wider range than can be used for conventional cookery is suitable because even paper and some plastics will do. Clear, heat-proof glass, glass ceramic, many kinds of plastic (provided they can withstand the heat generated in the food and don't have tight-fitting lids), specialist microware, paper, straw, wood, cooking bags, can all be used.

You can conduct a simple test to check if your existing, undecorated, non-metallic containers are suitable to use in a microwave oven. Put about 300 ml (½ pint) of water in a glass jug by the dish you wish to check. Microwave

A wide range of microware is now available, from high density plastics (left), to Pyrex and white porcelain (above).

for one minute on full power. If the dish remains cool to the touch, it can be used for cooking in the microwave. If it becomes warm, it is absorbing some of the microwave energy and this will slow down cooking. It might eventually damage the dish.

Capacity

Do not overfill, particularly when cooking food that is liquid or sloppy. Only half-fill when the food being cooked is likely to boil up and overspill – this is roughly the same as with conventional methods, for example milk-based liquids, high-sugar content fruity desserts and jams, starchy items such as parsnips, potatoes, etc. Cakes and puddings must have plenty of space to rise, as they will spill over as soon as the mixture reaches the rim.

Large pieces of food such as whole fish, apples and chicken pieces, which are mainly cooked dry, should be placed in a dish in which they fit tightly, leaving no large gap at either end. When cooking in a small amount of sauce or gravy, this is even more important, as the seeped liquid will dry around the inside edges. This is also a factor when thawing food in the microwave oven.

Shape

High-sided dishes should be chosen when extremely high temperatures are likely to occur, for example when making a brown roux. High sides shield the food so that the risk of burning is lessened. Shallow dishes hasten cooking times because the microwaves can get through the food more quickly. Even-shaped dishes with rounded corners should be chosen when round shapes are not suitable.

Materials

The material must be selected carefully. Few dishes are grill- or flame-proof (Corning Ware is one of the few which are). When foods can be browned at a distance from the grill, for example cakes and crumbles, this is less important. Never use plastics or paper for dishes finished in this way. Follow the manufacturer's instructions whenever special microware is used. For example, some Ovenable Board is resistant to 200°C/400°F, Gas Mark 6 in a conventional oven, while others are only able to withstand 180°C/350°F, Gas Mark 4. Some plastics can also be used in the conventional oven if they have a high temperature tolerance but this is again subject to the manufacturer's instructions. Never attempt to cook high-fat or high-sugar content foods in plastics unless the manufacturer specifically recommends this.

Using metal

As microwaves are reflected by metal, generally speaking metal cannot be used in a microwave oven. Solid or thick metals such as stainless steel prevent the microwaves from reaching the food and therefore from cooking it. Anything with a metal trim, metallic coloured inscriptions, or flimsy material such as silver paper, will cause sparking and may damage the magnetron which is the most expensive part of the oven to replace. Objects such as metal staples, pins or tags, normally used to seal polythene bags, are dangerous to use. In certain circumstances where the metal is dense, for example a skewer, provided it is pressed well into the food and the mass of food is greater than that of the metal, it will be safe. However, when metal skewers are used for such items as kebabs, the parts of the food close to the skewers will remain uncooked.

Another kind of metal that you cannot use in the microwave oven is a tin or can even if it is opened – it is no use trying to heat your baked beans in the can.

In no circumstances should metal touch the top or sides of the oven. The bottom of the oven is always protected by a fixed shelf or removable turntable.

The browning dish or plate

This accessory deserves special mention for it is invaluable when foods such as chops and steaks require searing or sealing. I would describe browning dishes and plates more as sealing than browning devices, but when used correctly, a good degree of browning can be obtained to give the food the look of 'conventional cooking'. The dishes are most useful for browning foods to which a sauce or other ingredients will later be added. The lid can be put on at that stage and cooking continues in the usual way.

The browning plates are often designed with a channel to catch any residual fats and these really produce good brown results. No juices rest on the surface to inhibit the browning process.

To brown or sear food, place these special microwave utensils empty in the microwave oven and set the oven to full power for a few minutes. The base has a special coating on the underside which absorbs the microwaves, it becomes extremely hot and reaches a temperature of 315°C/600°F. In so doing the surface turns yellow but reverts to its normal white colour when cool.

The browning dish only retains this very high temperature for a short time. Have the food to be sealed ready to put into it because the surface heat diminishes. Subsequent cooking should follow immediately.

Using aluminium foil

There are, however, instances where metal can be utilized in the microwave oven. Provided you follow directions, aluminium foil can safely be used. Its main advantage is in covering food to prevent overcooking. Prepared frozen foods are sometimes packed in foil containers with foil lids. If these containers are no deeper than 2 cm (¾ in), there is no need to transfer the food into another dish. Remove the lid of the foil container and replace the container in the cardboard packet, then microwave to cook or reheat. If foil touches the sides of the oven the magnetron will be damaged and the metal linings pitted.

Whenever foil is used to shield food to prevent overcooking it should be applied sparingly and be smoothed as flat as possible. If foil pierces food or sticks up in a point, burning can result. This is infrequent but possible, so do look out for it. If you are using foil in an oven where there is a considerable movement of air, due to a fan or cooling system, fix the foil with wooden cocktail sticks. Foil can be placed underneath the plastic or paper cover or lid, thus avoiding any contact with the sides of the oven. For example, when roasting a chicken in a roasting bag, tuck pieces of foil around the wing tips and legs half-way through cooking, inside the bag.

Where food cooked in the microwave can be stirred it is easy to obtain even results. When food cannot be stirred, for example a cake, the shape of the dish becomes very important. If you want to make a loaf-shaped cake, you may find that the ends of the cake cook quickly, while the centre part remains undercooked. When this stage is reached, smooth foil over the two cooked ends, leaving the middle exposed to the microwave energy. The centre will soon catch up and the cake will be evenly cooked.

Browning dishes are a definite boon to meat cookery; some microwave ovens have built-in browning devices.

Tenting

Another use for foil is for tenting during standing times. Since cooking continues after the food is removed from the microwave oven, it is a good idea to cover or enclose the dish with foil to keep in as much heat as possible. This is known as tenting. By using this method, you not only save electricity but you can cook in sequence ensuring that all parts of the meal are ready at the same time. Tenting produces the best results when used for the longer-cooking items such as a joint of meat. It does not matter which side of the foil is innermost.

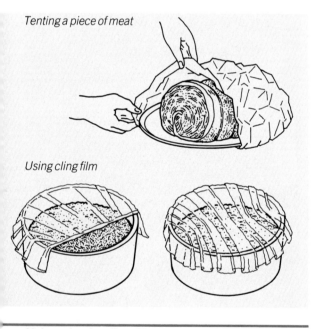

Tenting a piece of meat

Using cling film

Using plastic cling film

This material can play a major part in microwave cookery. It makes an excellent lid whenever you wish to use a dish for which you have no cover (however, special plastic lids are now available from microware suppliers). Because cling film holds in the heat, it can also be used to speed up the cooking process. But be careful when removing it as steam can give a nasty scald if you don't protect your hands (and face). Some books recommend slitting the film when applying it over dishes before cooking but I have never needed to. Always remove it from the side farthest away from you.

The film should be loosely applied with plenty of wrinkles or pleats so there will then be enough 'give' to prevent it bursting. You may see it balloon up during cooking, but it will subside as soon as the dish is removed from the microwave oven. The cling film should not be in direct contact with the food or the heat from the food may cause it to melt. As the cling film is transparent, the food can be watched during cooking and if the film is left in position after cooking is completed, it will form a protective seal.

If the food needs to be stirred during cooking, it is best to cover it partially with the cling film, leaving a gap through which a spoon can slide for easy stirring. Cling film cannot be easily repositioned once the cooking has started.

Cling film is also useful for lining dishes prior to cooking. This may help eliminate smells such as those in strongly flavoured casseroles or in tomato sauces which can taint or stain plastic microwave containers.

The food

There is no doubt that good quality ingredients produce the best results. Inevitably a fresh chicken will cook more succulently than a frozen bird and fresh fish better than stale. When shopping for items which will not subsequently be cut up, try to choose even sizes. For example, if you have decided to cook four trout, it is better to buy four equal-sized fish than two larger and two smaller, because the smaller ones will cook more quickly and you will have to remove them from the dish before the others are ready.

When even-shaped foodstuffs are not obtainable, arrange the items in the dish with the larger pieces on the outside. If vegetables, meat or other comestibles need to be cut up before cooking, for example sliced carrots or lamb for curry, slice or divide the pieces uniformly. Spread food out to an even thickness in the dish and unless the food is in a thin liquid, try to leave a gap in the middle. It should then cook more evenly.

A-Z of Hints and Recipes

NB Nearly all the recently manufactured microwave ovens offer a choice of power levels. In this chart we have used three settings – low, medium and full. Please refer to the chart on page 14 for relative settings.

Bread

Cut loaves
To thaw: leave in wrapping. Microwave on low for 5 minutes. If only few slices required, microwave on full power for 20 seconds until ends give, then remove the slices at either end. Return remainder to freezer.

Loaves
To thaw: wrap in kitchen paper. Microwave on high only until hard lump remains inside (2 minutes). Overthawing causes them to go stale quickly.
To make: warm flour in microwave on full power for 15 seconds. Assist proving by heating on low for 15 seconds every 10 minutes. Bread can be cooked in microwave, but the texture is close without a crisp brown crust. Best cooked on three-quarters power. Brown is more successful than white bread. *Possible timing* 8 minutes.

Rolls
To thaw: microwave in paper but not plastic bags on low (8 seconds each).

Tea breads
To thaw: microwave on full power as for loaves.
To cook: more successful to bake two small loaf shapes than one long. Use dark ingredients, e.g. treacle and brown sugar. Breads will be brown inside, pale outside. Cook half on full power, half on low. *Possible timing* Times will depend on ingredients. Approx. 7 minutes.

Cakes and biscuits

Bar cookies
To thaw: high sugar content items thaw readily at room temperature.
To cook: microwave on full power. Watch carefully so that

cookies do not burn. Test with wooden cocktail stick.
Possible timing 3 minutes.

Cheesecake

To thaw: thaw uncovered on low.
To make: for refrigerator cheesecake use microwave short-cut to dissolve gelatine. Baked cheesecake, choose even-shaped dish, not in excess of 23cm (9in). Cook on full power for 1 minute, then complete cooking on low. Remove from microwave when centre is only just set. Decorate when cold. *Possible timing* 12 minutes.

Christmas cake

To thaw: thaw on low until outside edges feel pliant. Leave at room temperature to complete thawing.
To cook: best cooked on low which gives time for fruit flavours to develop. Do not overcook. Wrap in foil and leave for a few days before serving. A quick cake can be made on

Fruit cakes can be successfully microwaved.

Xmas morning using a savarin ring. Press commercial marzipan over surface while the cake is still warm, then leave to cool before applying royal icing. *Possible timing* 40 minutes.

Doughnuts
To thaw: stand on kitchen paper. Microwave on full power for 5 to 10 seconds only. Leave to stand for a few minutes to allow jam to cool slightly.

Fruit cake
To thaw: as for Christmas cake (see page 27).

Recipe: Fruit cake
Put 75g (3oz/⅓ cup) butter in large bowl. Microwave on full power 10 to 15 seconds until softened. Beat in 75g (3oz/½ cup) soft brown sugar. Add 125g (4oz/1 cup) plain sifted flour, 2 level teaspoons baking powder, 1 level teaspoon mixed spice, 25g (1oz/¼ cup) ground almonds and 2 large beaten eggs. Mix in 1 teaspoon liquid caramel or gravy browning and 1 teaspoon golden syrup. Stir in 3 to 4 tablespoons milk to soft dropping consistency. Finally add 175g (6oz/1 cup) mixed dried fruit and 5 chopped glacé cherries. Fill a greased and lined cake shape. Microwave at full power. Turn the dish through 90° four times during cooking. Bake until the cake is just dry on top. Turn out and when cool, wrap in cling film or foil. Store for a few days for flavour to develop. *Possible timing* 5 minutes on full power or 14 on low.

Kugelhopf
To thaw: microwave on full power for few seconds only.
To make: use microwave for warming flour as for bread (see page 26) and to hasten proving. Use a suitable kugelhopf ring. Cook on full power. *Possible timing* 4 minutes.

Large cakes
To thaw: thaw on low until the sides feel pliable. Then complete thawing at room temperature.
To make: do not butter the pans too thickly. Some pans (e.g. plastic) require no greasing at all. After cooking, some cakes may be moist round the edges — this is probably

because of the composition of the dish used. Try a different one next time. Microwave cooking will not produce a crust on cakes and the top outer layer will feel soft. This is not a sign of under-cooking. If the cake is turned out on to a wire rack, the top and sides should dry off and the cake can then be reversed by pressing gently through the wire to prevent the top surface from coming away. Choose ring shapes for even cooking results. *Possible timing* 6 minutes.

Rum babas
To thaw: microwave on low until thawed, but still cold, approximately 1 minute.
To make: mixture cooks well in microwave in small cups. Warm flour and hasten proving as for bread (see page 26).

Sandwich cakes
To thaw: thaw for brief period on full power.
To cook: shallow straight-sided containers can be bought from specialist shops. As cakes do not brown in the microwave, put yellow colouring in the mixture. Also add some dairy butter flavouring as the cake cooks so quickly, it does not give an opportunity for the flavours to develop, hence use butter rather than margarine in the mixture. Cook each layer of the cake separately. *Possible timing* 2 minutes each.

Savarin
To thaw: microwave on low until thawed but still cold (approximately 1 minute).
To cook: warm flour and hasten proving as for bread (see page 26). Use large ring. The syrup can also be cooked in the microwave. *Possible timing* 10 minutes.

Shortbread
To thaw: microwave on low for 15 to 20 seconds.

Recipe: Shortbread
Rub 125g (4oz/½cup) unsalted butter into 175g (6oz/1½cups) self-raising flour, stir in 50g (2oz/⅓cup) demerara sugar. Press mixture into dish which should be 15-18cm (6-7in) in diameter. Try using a stacking ring on non-stick paper, as it is difficult to serve from a dish with a

fixed base. If no ring available, freeze, then turn out and thaw. No need to grease dish. Cook on full power and cut into wedges before completely cold. Test with wooden cocktail stick, which should come out clean. When cooked, shortbread should be light brown inside so do not overcook. *Possible timing* 4 minutes.

Special muffin pans are available from microwave suppliers – ideal for small cakes.

Small cakes

To thaw: thaw on full power. Single cakes need 10 seconds. If thawed in batches, spread out on shelf and reposition during thawing.

To cook: use either double paper cases or single cases placed in muffin pans (specialized cake microware). Arrange the cakes in a circle but do not put one in the middle. Reposition during cooking. Only a few at a time can be cooked, as with biscuits. *Possible timing* 15 seconds per cake.

Confectionery, icings and frostings

American frosting
To thaw: icings cannot be completely frozen because of their high sugar content, but they will congeal without freezing solid. Will thaw rapidly at room temperature; if too solid to spread, microwave on low for few seconds.

Recipe: American frosting
Stir 250 g (8 oz/1 cup) sugar, pinch cream of tartar and 4 tablespoons water together in a heat-resistant jug (e.g. Pyrex). Bring to boil without stirring until large bubbles form and remove from oven before colour changes. While doing this whisk egg white until stiff, pour the syrup in a thin stream on to the egg white while beating until the mixture turns to a thick frosting. *Possible timing* 4 minutes.

Caramel
Not suitable for freezing.
To cook: blend sugar and water in quantity according to the result required. The more water, the longer cooking takes. Watch carefully as the bubbles get larger and larger. Once the syrup has started to darken, it will do so rapidly, so remove when mid-brown. Always cook in a tall Pyrex measuring jug to lessen chances of the caramel boiling over. Stirring causes the syrup to crystallize though stirring only once will delay excessive bubbling. *Possible timing* 2 minutes after boiling.

Chocolate
Freeze left-over chocolate in container, then scrape out and finely chop. No need to thaw before use as decoration.
To melt: microwave on full power until just softened, but maintaining its shape. The remainder will melt when you stir the mixture. Chocolate can burn inside and this is less likely if you stir during melting. Don't melt in anything that could scar or mark. Plain chocolate melts more evenly than milk chocolate. Chocolate chips can also be melted in the microwave oven. *Possible timing* 1 minute plus.

Fudge

Thaws quickly at room temperature.

To cook: because milk may boil over, use a large bowl that will be resistant to very high temperatures. Make sure you use oven gloves. If the mixture bubbles over, switch to a low setting for a few seconds, then switch back to full power. Chocolate fudge provides a smoother result than vanilla fudge. *Possible timing* 12 minutes for 500 g (1 lb).

Praline

To make: use a plate which is resistant to very high temperatures. Spread the mixture on a double sheet of non-stick paper and stir frequently. As each area melts, this should be mixed with the remainder using a wooden spoon, otherwise there will be one central burning patch which would catch fire. Never leave cooking unattended. Switch off oven while praline is still mid-brown as it will get darker. Cannot be lifted off oven shelf until cold, then it can be broken up, ground or crushed. *Possible timing* Depends on quantity. Minimum 5 minutes.

Sugar syrup

To thaw: might have crusty topping when removed from freezer which merely requires mixing in.

Recipe: Sugar syrup

250 g (8 oz/1 cup) granulated sugar to 150 ml (5 fl oz/ ⅔ cup) water. Cook in Pyrex or similar large bowl. Microwave for 2½ minutes on full power, stir, then continue for 2 minutes after syrup boils, when temperature reaches 105°C/215°F. Store in screw-top jar when cool. *Possible timing* 4½ minutes.

Dairy Produce

Butter

To melt from frozen: unwrap block and put in dish; microwave on low until edges droop. Scrape softened butter off two ends and leave remainder to thaw at room temperature. Satisfactory to melt up to 75 g (3 oz/⅓ cup) from refrigerator.

To soften from frozen: unwrap block and put in dish;

microwave on low. *Possible timing* ½ minute for 50g
(2oz/¼ cup).
To clarify: cover with greaseproof paper to prevent spitting.
Possible timing 1 minute for 50g (2oz/¼ cup).

Cheese, fondue

To thaw: microwave on full power for 4 minutes, turning
through 90° after each minute.
To cook: microwave on low until cheese is melted, then
stabilize with cornflour blended with kirsch, stir into
cheese and cook until bubbling. *Possible timing* 10
minutes.

Cheese, grated

To thaw: grated cheese freezes well provided it is not
compacted. Thaw at room temperature, or use without
prior thawing.
To cook: do not add grated cheese to frozen dishes which
are to be reheated. Thaw them first. Cheese attracts the
microwaves and would cook before the dish has begun to
thaw and would become stringy.
To melt cheese: must be done on low.

Cheese soufflé

To cook: only half-fill dishes as considerable rising possible. Not very good with pulsing low power, but if your
oven has continuous low power, soufflés are possible.
Possible timing 30 minutes.

Cheese Recipe: Welsh rarebit

Mix approximately 75g (3oz/¾ cup) grated Cheddar
cheese with a pinch of mustard powder, black pepper and
a level teaspoon of cornflour. Stir in 2 tablespoons milk.
Microwave on low power for 2 minutes or until the cheese
has just melted. Stir in a further 50g (2oz/½ cup) grated
Cheddar cheese. Pile on two slices of hot buttered toast,
then brown under a preheated grill. *Possible timing* 2
minutes.

Cream, double

To thaw: only whipped double cream may be frozen and
should be fractionally thawed at the lowest possible setting

or it will separate.

To cook: double cream reacts similarly in a microwave oven and a conventional one.

Eggs

To thaw: Yolks – defrost at room temperature. Whites – initially defrost in container at low setting until just liquified around edges. Ready as soon as consistency of melting snow is reached. Stir well.

To cook: do not cook in shells; they will explode.

To coddle: place water in a container (glass or jug is suitable) and bring to the boil in the microwave. Remove from oven, immerse the egg in the water and cover tightly with cling film. No further cooking is necessary.

To fry: break the egg into a preheated browning dish to which a generous knob of butter has been added during the last half minute. Quickly pierce the yolk, then cover with the lid and microwave on full power. It is best to undercook as the egg continues cooking during standing time. *Possible timing* After adding to browning dish, 20 seconds. Allow standing time before uncovering.

To hard-cook: cook whites and yolks separately. Cook yolks on low setting in narrow, covered, greased container. Lightly stir. Cook until just opaque, uncover and chop when cool. *Possible timing* 5 minutes. Cook whites on low setting in narrow, covered, greased container, stirring 3 times until just set. Leave to stand 3 minutes before removing cover. Chop when cool. *Possible timing* 2 minutes.

To poach: Method A – using microwave egg poachers. Break the eggs into the buttered poachers, puncture the yolks lightly. Cover each poacher with cling film. Cook on medium, turning the dishes through 180° once during cooking. Remove cling film, leave to stand for a minute before serving. Always undercook. *Possible timing* 30 seconds for 1 egg, 20 seconds for more than 1 egg cooked simultaneously.

Method B – eggs poached in water. Half-fill a small dish with boiling water. Add pinch salt or drop of vinegar. Bring back to the boil in the microwave oven using full power. Swirl the water with a spoon handle and break in the egg. Partially cover and microwave on medium. Allow a standing time before serving. *Possible timing* 15 to 30 seconds

Preparing poached eggs and scrambled eggs.

per egg.
To scramble: put a knob of butter in a narrow container or
Pyrex bowl and microwave at full power until it has melted.
Add 2 beaten eggs, 2 tablespoons cold water, pinch of salt
and pepper. Microwave at full power stirring every 30
seconds. Cook until just set and leave to stand for 1 to 2
minutes before serving. *Possible timing* 1½ to 2 minutes
for 2-egg portions.

Margarine, hard
To thaw: thaw as for butter (see page 32).

Milk
To thaw: only homogenized milk should be frozen. Thaw
on low, stirring frequently.

To heat from cold: 1 l (1¾pt/4¼ cups) *Possible timing* 7 to 8 minutes to steaming point.

150 ml (¼pt/⅔ cup) *Possible timing* 1½ minutes to boiling.

300 ml (½pt/1¼ cups) *Possible timing* 2½ minutes to boiling.

600 ml (1 pt/2½ cups) *Possible timing* 4 minutes to boiling.

Heat for the minimum time recommended, then check for required temperature. Do not heat liquids in tall narrow bottles, such as milk bottles. Small amounts of liquid are better left uncovered during reheating. Where there is a medium setting, milk and milk-based drinks should be cooked at this speed, increase the heating timings by one-third.

Drinks and liquids

Chocolate

To heat: drinks should be heated to 60-65°C/140-150°F. A cup can be filled to the brim if it is only to be heated to this temperature. If liquid is to be boiled leave at least 1 cm (½in) at the top. An occasional gentle stir during heating prevents liquids from boiling over. If several cups are being heated at once, arrange them in a circle on the oven shelf. *Possible timing* 1 cup 1 minute on full power.

Coffee, black

To heat: 1 cup *Possible timing* 1¾ minutes.

2 cups *Possible timing* 3 minutes.

4 cups *Possible timing* 5 minutes.

Flambéed dishes

To heat alcohol: warm brandy or similar spirits in a heat-proof cup or glass in the microwave oven for a few seconds, then ignite and pour over the cooked dish. *Possible timing* 7 seconds on full power.

Recipe:
Mulled wine

Mix 750 ml (1¼pt/3 cups) red wine, 12 cloves, 2 small pieces of cinnamon, the grated rind and juice of a lemon and an orange in a large bowl and cook on full power until

nearly boiling. Strain into another bowl which has been
heated, add sugar to taste and serve warm. *Possible timing*
5 minutes.

Water

To boil: tap container on work surface before heating to
knock out air bubbles.
150 ml (¼pt/⅔ cup) *Possible timing* 1¾ minutes to boiling.
200 ml (⅓pt/⅞ cup) *Possible timing* 2¼ minutes to boiling.
300 ml (½pt/1¼ cups) *Possible timing* 3¼ minutes to
boiling.
600 ml (1 pt/2½ cups) *Possible timing* 6 minutes to
boiling.

Fish and seafood

Clams and scallops

To thaw: defrost in the original wrapper if suitable, remembering to slash sealed bags first. Put the package in a
shallow dish to catch any liquid. Thaw on a low setting
allowing 8 to 10 minutes per 500 g (1 lb). Leave to stand at
room temperature for an equal amount of time, then rinse
well under cold water to complete defrosting.
To cook: do not cook from the frozen state. Remove wrapping and rinse under cold water, then pat dry with kitchen
paper. Arrange in a single layer in a shallow dish and
reposition half-way through cooking. Cook covered to retain the moisture and season before cooking. Fish cooks
quickly because of its high moisture content. Do not overcook. The coral on scallops, being enclosed in a skin, may
pop during cooking. If preferred, pierce these first before
cooking. Large scallops can be cut in half. *Possible timing*
6 minutes cooking time plus 2 minutes standing time.

Cutlets or steaks

To thaw: these vary in size but the usual commercially
frozen weight is 125 g (4 oz). Cover lightly with greaseproof
paper, microwave on low power for 4 minutes, giving the
dish a turn through 180° after 2 minutes. Allow to stand for
5 minutes before continuing to cook.
To cook: season the fish and place in a shallow dish. Cook
covered. If 1 or 2 are being cooked, turn the cutlets over

half-way through cooking. For 4 or more, reposition half-way through cooking, and give the dish a turn through 180° half-way through this period. Cutlets which have a bone in the middle tend to splatter. Allow a standing time for these.
Possible timing 4 minutes per 500g (1 lb) cooking time, followed by 2 to 3 minutes standing time.

Fillets, white

To thaw: solid blocks should be turned over half-way through defrosting. Separate the pieces as soon as it is possible. Allow 6 minutes per 500g (1 lb). If the fillets are not defrosted by this time, rinse them under cold water. Sometimes frozen fish fillets produce a large amount of liquid. If the fillets are to be served with a sauce, then use it, otherwise drain away surplus fluid before cooking.

To cook: season the fillets and arrange in a shallow dish with the tails towards the centre. It is important to have the fish at an equal thickness so you may prefer to overlap the tails. However, this makes it more difficult to separate for serving. Turn the dish through 180° half-way through cooking. Allow a standing time of 2 minutes before un-

covering. Small fillets or half fillets can be rolled up and arranged in a circle in the dish (a savarin ring is useful). *Possible timing* 4 minutes per 500g (1lb) stuffed or unstuffed.

Fish fingers
To thaw: fish fingers are one of the few types of fish which do not need to be thawed before cooking continues.
To cook: place the number required on a buttered plate and leave uncovered or cover only lightly. Reposition and turn over half-way through cooking. Fish fingers may be cooked in a shallow dish in a tablespoon of cooking oil. This will give a fried appearance. The browning dish also produces good results. *Possible timing* 10 fish fingers — 3 minutes from frozen.

Fish, whole
To thaw: microwave on low power allowing 8 to 12 minutes per 500g (1lb). Turn the dish through 180° half-way

Fish cooked to perfection – moist and delicious.

through the given time. Thaw small fish in a dish. Thaw large fish in an unsealed roaster bag. Shield head and tail ends with aluminium foil if they become warm to the touch. Do not overthaw. It is better to complete thawing in cold water.

To cook: small whole fish can be cooked in a dish placing them head to tail. Microwave covered with greaseproof paper. Slash the skin in two or three places to prevent bursting. Large whole fish must be cooked curved. If necessary, tie round with string. Whole fish may be cooked either on full power or on defrost multiplying the cooking time by 2½. If cooking on medium, multiply the cooking time by 1¾. *Possible timing* 4 minutes per 500g (1lb).

Herrings

Herrings can be cooked from frozen.

To cook: cut off the heads, gut and clean. Can be cooked whole, boned, folded and stuffed as flat fillets, or rolled up. When cooked whole or folded, score the skin in 2 or 3 places with a sharp knife. Arrange whole fish head to tail in a shallow dish and turn over half-way through cooking. Cook covered with greased paper or the fish skin may adhere. Most conventional herring recipes can be adapted, with the exception of frying. Cook on full power. *Possible timing* 4 minutes per 500g (1lb).

Kippers

To thaw: put pack on a plate and slit across the top. Defrost on full power, turning the dish through 180° half-way through the cooking time. Home-frozen kippers should be frozen flat.

To cook: (packaged kippers from frozen), put package on plate and slit top. Defrost and cook in one stage on full power. Small pack will take 4 minutes, large pack 7 minutes. Leave to stand 2 minutes before removing from bag. Reduce the time by one-third if fish starts from refrigeration temperature. Fresh kippers are best cooked 1 or 2 at a time. Arrange singly or tails overlapping in centre of dish, skin sides down. Cover loosely with cling film. Turn the dish once during cooking. Leave for approximately 2 minutes before carefully removing cling film. *Possible timing* 3½ minutes per 500g (1lb).

Large centre cuts of whole fish

To thaw: cover with greaseproof paper and thaw on low setting. Carefully turn dish 4 times during defrosting so that all sections are thawed at an equal rate. Thaw until the outside is pliable, then complete the process under cold water. Leave to stand to completely thaw before cooking. Allow 8 to 12 minutes per 500 g (1 lb) giving the dish a 180° turn half-way through the cooking.

To cook: score the skin 2 or 3 times, season, butter and cover with greaseproof paper before cooking. Turn over and reposition at least once during cooking. Allow a 4-minute standing time before serving. *Possible timing* 4 to 5 minutes per 500 g (1 lb).

Large piece tail end

To thaw: score skin with a sharp knife. Place in shallow dish. Cover with greaseproof paper. Defrost on low setting. Turn the dish 3 or 4 times during defrosting. Smooth a small piece of aluminium foil over the thin end of the fish as soon as this part is thawed. Leave to stand to complete defrosting. Allow 6 minutes per 500 g (1 lb).

To cook: cook covered with greaseproof paper on full power. Turn thick fish over half-way through cooking. Shield thin ends with a small piece of smoothed aluminium foil as soon as these parts are cooked. When cooking in butter melt and heat it first. Leave to stand for at least 3 minutes before serving. *Possible timing* 4 to 5 minutes per 500 g (1 lb).

Lobster

To thaw: put (uncooked) lobster in a shallow dish with the pale side uppermost. A lobster weighing 750 g (1½ lb) will take about 15 minutes to defrost. Place in a shallow dish and microwave on low power for 8 minutes, turning the dish through 180° half-way through this time. Turn the lobster over and then repeat the process. Check during defrosting and if any of the thinner parts feel warm to the touch, shield these with a small, smooth piece of aluminium foil, making sure that it does not touch the sides of the oven. Remove while still slightly icy and leave to complete thawing at room temperature until the lobster feels pliable. Treat cooked frozen lobster similarly.

To cook: kill live lobster before cooking. Place raw lobster in a shallow dish with the black sides down. Add 8 or 9 tablespoons hot water. Cover loosely with cling film. Microwave on full power, turning the lobster over and also turning the dish through 180° half-way through cooking. Leave to stand for 5 minutes before serving. The meat should be translucent in the centre. Cooking will be completed during the standing time. Cook only until the shell has turned to red. Overcooking causes toughening. To use frozen lobster remove the meat from the shell and then use in a suitable recipe. *Possible timing* 5 to 8 minutes per 500 g (1 lb) on full power depending upon the overall size.

Lobster tails (uncooked)

To thaw: place in a shallow dish with the pale underside uppermost. Use kitchen paper to support them. Microwave on low power for 8 to 10 minutes per 500 g (1 lb), turn the pieces over halfway through defrosting, leave to stand for 5 minutes to complete defrosting. When completely thawed, the lobster tails should feel cool but be pliable.

To cook: arrange in a shallow dish with the underside uppermost. Seven-eighths cover with cling film. Half-way through the cooking time take the tails out of the dish and split through the back of the shell, but do not sever underneath. Open out the tails and replace in the dish flesh side uppermost. Brush with melted butter and sprinkle with lemon juice. Re-cover and microwave on full power for the second part of the given time, when the shell will be bright red and the lobster meat pink. Do not overcook. Leave to stand 5 minutes before serving. *Possible timing* 7 minutes per 500 g (1 lb).

Plaice

To thaw: thaw whole plaice in a shallow dish covered with greaseproof paper. Defrost on low power, turning the dish 4 times during defrosting. Shield the tail with a smooth piece of aluminium foil as soon as this part is thawed. Plaice fillets should be thawed in a single layer with the tails overlapping.

To cook: remove head and dark skin if preferred or slash the skin with a sharp knife. Season well, cover and microwave on full power, turning the dish 4 times during cooking. To produce a better flavour, sprinkle the fish with salt and pepper and coat with flour. Melt 50 g (2 oz/¼ cup) butter in a shallow dish in the microwave oven, put plaice in the dish and turn to coat both sides with butter. Cover with greaseproof paper and microwave on full power, turning the fish over and turning the dish through 180° half-way through cooking. After testing, cover and leave to stand for 3 minutes before serving. *Possible timing* 4 minutes per 500 g (1 lb); 5 minutes for sautéing.

Prawns and shrimps

To cook: these are usually sold ready cooked and sometimes unpeeled. Small varieties to be included in cooked dishes may be used direct from the freezer packet. To thaw for use in salads, arrange in a circle on a dish lined with kitchen paper. Microwave on low power for half the given time, then shake the dish to rearrange and microwave for the remaining time. Shellfish should feel pliable but cool. There is no need to cover. Allow approximately 5 minutes per 500 g (1 lb) on low setting.

Salmon steaks (see page 44).

To cook or heat: arrange in a single layer in a shallow dish. Seven-eighths cover with cling film. Microwave on full power for half the given time, then stir sides to middle. Cook on full power. Raw, peeled shrimps will turn pink and opaque when cooked. Leave to stand for 1 to 2 minutes before removing the cling film. *Possible timing* 5 minutes per 500 g (1 lb).

Roes
To thaw: best to thaw unwrapped in the refrigerator.
To cook: because fish roes are enclosed in a skin, they tend to spatter during cooking. Cover completely and shake the dish during cooking to reposition. Do not overcook and do not uncover until a standing time of 3 to 4 minutes has elapsed. *Possible timing* 4 minutes per 500 g (1 lb).

Salmon
To thaw: it is essential to thaw salmon completely before cooking. Feel the cutlets of salmon. The temperature in the middle must be the same as that on the outside or cooking will be uneven. To thaw thin pieces, place in a shallow dish, then turn over and reposition half-way through defrosting. As soon as the outside edges are pliable, complete thawing under cold water. Whole fish or large middle cuts – turn over half-way through the defrosting time. Complete thawing under cold water.
To cook salmon steaks: arrange thin ends towards the centre in a shallow dish covered with greaseproof paper. Alternatively, cook in a court bouillon or dip in seasoned flour and cook in melted butter in a preheated browning dish. *Large pieces:* Score the skin in 2 or 3 places, microwave on full or low power, allowing 2½ times as long when cooking on low power. Turn over half-way through cooking. Microwave covered with greaseproof paper; allow a standing time of 4 minutes before serving. *Possible timing* 4 minutes per 500 g (1 lb) on full power.

Salmon trout
To thaw: defrost on low setting until the surface yields to gentle pressure. Then complete thawing under cold water.
To cook: the easiest way is to cook the fish curved in a large round shallow dish. The fish cannot be straightened out

after cooking. Make 2 or 3 slits in the skin to prevent bursting and cook covered with greaseproof paper. Small fish can be placed diagonally on the oven shelf. Cook in an unsealed roasting bag covering the head and tail with smoothed foil as soon as these parts are cooked. The foil must not touch the sides of the oven. If preferred, microwave on low allowing 2½ times the given time. *Possible timing* 4 minutes per 500 g (1 lb) depending on the thickness of the fish.

Smoked haddock

To thaw: thaw in the cooking dish. Choose a dish into which the fish just fits. Cover with cling film. Microwave on low until the spine is no longer glassy. Turn the dish several times during defrosting. The centre of large smoked haddock are sometimes difficult to defrost without the thin part of the tail and the sides beginning to cook. Should this start to happen, leave the fish at room temperature until the colour is even. Smoked haddock and cod fillets are easier to thaw by microwave because of their more even shape and lack of bone.

To cook: add 2 tablespoons water to very salty fish. Less smoked and salty fish require no additional water. Cover very loosely with cling film. Turn the dish through 90° 4 times during cooking. For fillets, cut into even shapes and reposition once during cooking. Cook on full power. *Possible timing* 4 minutes per 500 g (1 lb).

Sole, Dover

To thaw: thaw gently on low, giving a 5-minute rest half-way through the defrosting period. This is important because of the shape of this delicate fish. Turn the dish through 90° 4 times during defrosting and complete under cold water as soon as the fish is pliable. Allow 6 minutes per 500 g (1 lb).

To cook: if the fish is very cold when starting to cook, microwave on low, allowing 6 to 8 minutes per 500 g (1 lb). Fish which is barely cold to the touch may be cooked on full power. Trim the fish and remove the dark skin. If cooking more than one fish, place head to tail, side by side in a long shallow dish. Dot with butter and sprinkle with salt and pepper. Three-quarters cover with cling film and microwave on full power giving the dish a turn through 90° 4 times during cooking. Do not cook more than 2 at a time. If 4 are required, slightly undercook each pair, then reheat allowing 45 seconds to 1 minute for each fish. When cooked the flesh of sole is firm. Overcooking will cause toughening. *Possible timing* 4 minutes per 500 g (1 lb).

Trout, whole

To thaw: slit the plastic package on top and then place in a dish. If more than 1 trout is being thawed, remove from the packaging and place head to tail in a single layer in a dish into which they just fit. Cover with greaseproof paper. Microwave on low allowing 8 minutes per 500 g (1 lb). Give the dish a turn through 180° half-way through the given time. Complete thawing under cold water.

To cook: gut and clean, then score the skin in 2 or 3 places. Arrange head to tail in a single layer and cover with grease-proof paper. Microwave on full power, then leave for 4 to 5 minutes before serving. Cook with or without stuffing as desired and include this in the total weight when calculating timing. Turn the dish through 90° 3 times during cooking. Test through the thickest part with the point of a knife — the flesh should flake easily. *Possible timing* 4 minutes per 500 g (1 lb).

Fish dishes

To cook: when extra ingredients are added to a fish dish and are to be cooked with the fish, for example a sauce or

Allow extra cooking time for added ingredients.

cooked vegetables, allow slightly longer cooking times. Use a dish that will just fit the length and width of the fish, if necessary choosing a deeper dish to accommodate the sauce. Always undercook fish dishes which are to be reheated. To remove fishy smells from the microwave oven, place left-over squeezed lemons with a few tablespoons of water in a large bowl or jug. Cover with greaseproof (wax) paper, microwave at full power for 1 to 2 minutes until boiling. Remove paper and leave the bowl in the switched-off oven for several minutes before removing.

Fruit

Apples

To thaw: for slices or quarters, place in a dish that will fit apple layers up to 2.5 cm (1 in) deep. Three-quarters cover and microwave on low, stirring from the sides to the middle twice during defrosting. Allow 6 minutes on low.

To cook: apple slices can be cooked from frozen but apple quarters are best thawed first because of their bulk. Stewed apples: add 75 g (3 oz/⅓ cup) sugar to 500 g (1 lb) prepared apples. Microwave on full power.

Recipe: Baked Apples

Core the apples and remove a sliver of the skin from the top and bottom. Score deeply round the waist. Large apples should be turned over once during cooking. Cook uncovered on full power, stuffing the apples according to your favourite recipe, and adding 1 to 2 tablespoons of water. Press filling well down into cavity. Cook for one-third of the given time, then turn the apple over. The top section will have turned to yellow but the bottom remains green. Continue microwaving until 1 cm (½ in) band of green is left in the centre, both top and bottom being yellow. Cover and leave to stand for 2 to 3 minutes or until the colour is uniform. The skins will remain tough. *Possible timing* 8 minutes per 500 g (1 lb) apple, 6 minutes per 4 apples.

Bananas

To cook: take care when cooking bananas in the microwave oven. They tend to discolour. Choose small bananas or cut them in half. Sauté in butter or cook in orange juice.

Recipe: Baked Bananas with Marmalade Sauce.
Combine 1 teaspoon lemon juice, 4 tablespoons of cold
water and ½ teaspoon cornflour in a large shallow dish.
Cook on full power for 1 minute. Blend in 6 tablespoons
orange marmalade or preserve and microwave on full
power for 2 to 3 minutes until the mixture boils. Mix in 25 g
(1 oz/2 tablespoons) unsalted butter. Add the bananas to
the dish and spoon the sauce over them. Microwave on full
power for 1 to 2 minutes, repositioning the bananas sides
to middle after 45 seconds. Bananas must be verging on
the under-ripe. *Possible timing* 20 seconds per banana.

Blackberries
To thaw: commercially frozen blackberries can be thawed
in the wrapping. Place on a plate and slit the top. Microwave on low power for 4 minutes each 300 g (10 oz/
2 cups), flexing the wrapping once or twice. Blackberries
can also be thawed on a high setting provided they are
frequently stirred and not covered. Too much stirring
causes fruit to break up. Only partially thaw, leaving at
room temperature to complete defrosting. To thaw frozen
blackberries, without the bag, follow the same procedure
but microwave covered.
To cook: use without further cooking in jam, crumbles or
jellies. Do not use frozen blackberries when making jellies
or the jelly will set unevenly round the fruit. *Possible timing*
5 minutes per 500 g (1 lb) on full power from frozen.

Blackcurrants, redcurrants and cranberries
To thaw: thaw in the wrapping as for blackberries (see
above) or empty the quantity required into a dish. Three-
quarters cover. Microwave on low power allowing 6
minutes per 500 g (1 lb), stirring 3 to 4 times during defrosting. Leave to stand for a few minutes at room temperature for even results. Do not overthaw.
To cook: layer this type of fruit 2.5-4 cm (1-1½ in) deep in a
suitable dish, adding 1 to 2 tablespoons of water. Three-
quarters cover with cling film and microwave on full power,
stirring occasionally. Add sugar later unless cooked with a
topping. These berries must be cooked covered to prevent
spattering. *Possible timing* 4 minutes per 500 g (1 lb) on
full power.

Citrus fruits (oranges, lemons, limes, grapefruit)

To thaw: arrange in a circle on the oven shelf. If only one piece is being defrosted it may be placed in the centre. Microwave on full power only until the peel becomes pliable, then leave to stand for 5 minutes. Overthawing results in cooked juice. Use frozen citrus slices in cold fruit punches, or iced drinks.

To cook: halved thawed citrus fruit is more difficult to juice because the skins tend to collapse. It is not possible to grate the zest.

Recipe: Baked Grapefruit

Halve and segment the grapefruit and space out on a large dish. Sprinkle with sugar and add a knob of butter. Microwave on full power. If desired, flavour with a little sweet sherry, brandy or Cointreau. *Possible timing* 1 minute per grapefruit half.

Dried fruit

To cook: generously cover with hot water, three-quarters cover, and cook on full power. Stir 3 or 4 times during cooking and leave to stand. Add sugar half-way through cooking period except for apricots, peaches and pears where the sugar should be added three-quarters of the way through cooking. *Possible timing* Per 500g (1 lb) with 600 ml (1 pt/2½ cups) water – 15 minutes plus 15 minutes standing time. Apricots should be stirred frequently as they dry and burn at the edges. To plump up small dried fruit for use in cakes, just cover with water or fruit juice. Cover and cook on full power for 5 minutes, stir once and leave to stand for 5 minutes. *Possible timing* 600 ml (1 pt/2½ cups) water for 250g (8 oz/1¼ cups) fruit – 20 minutes cooking time and 10 minutes standing.

Figs are best pre-soaked, put in a deep dish, covered with water and left for 2 hours before adding sugar. *Possible timing* Cover and cook for 10 minutes per 500g (1 lb), stirring occasionally.

Gooseberries

To thaw: place freezer bag on a plate, slash top and microwave on low 8 minutes per 500g (1 lb), flexing bag from time to time. Allow to stand at room temperature for 15 minutes to complete process. Alternatively turn required quantity into bowl, three-quarters cover and microwave on low, stirring occasionally. Can also be thawed on full power for 2 minutes, stirring and heating until thawed.

To cook: can be cooked from frozen by three-quarters covering to prevent spattering. Stir 2 or 3 times during cooking. Pierce the berries with a sharp knife. Frozen gooseberries take longer to soften but they cook more quickly than fresh fruit. *Possible timing* 8 minutes per 500 g (1 lb) on full power.

Nuts

To shell nuts: measure in volume by combining 2 bowls of nuts with 1 of water in a large casserole, microwave on full power.

Walnuts, pecan and brazils: *Possible timing* 3 minutes.

Chestnuts: slit and place 10 at a time on the oven shelf with a glass of water in the back of the oven and microwave on full power, stirring once, until skins are soft. Return to oven to re-soften if the skins go hard. *Possible timing* 4 minutes.

Salted almonds: place skinned nuts in large shallow dish, and microwave on full power, stirring occasionally. Sprinkle liberally with salt while still hot. Store in screw-top jar for up to 6 weeks. *Possible timing* 5 minutes.

Roasting shelled nuts: pile onto a double sheet of grease-proof paper and cook on full power, stirring frequently. To test, cut 1 or 2 nuts open and inspect them. Nuts may burn if cooked for too long. *Possible timing* 2 minutes per 125 g (4 oz/½ cup).

Pears

To thaw: the structure of pears is delicate so they should be handled as little as possible. Place them in a deep narrow container, cover and microwave on low. Allow 15 minutes to 500 g (1 lb). Turn the dish through 90° every 3 minutes. Do not attempt to separate the pears until the final part of the defrosting time to avoid any damage to the fruit. Leave to stand for 5 minutes before removing the cover. Pears frozen in a block should be placed in the dish, ice side up.

Pears in Red Wine.

Recipe: Baked Pears

Arrange halved, cored pears in a shallow dish, the stalk ends towards the centre. Dot with butter and sprinkle with sugar. Cover and microwave on full power, turning the dish through 180° half-way through cooking. Remove the cover but allow a 2-minute standing time. Do not overcook or pears will lose their firm texture. *Possible timing* 1 minute for each pear half.

Recipe: Pears in Red Wine

Combine 150 ml (¼ pt/⅔ cup) red wine with 50 g (2 oz/⅓ cup) demerara sugar in a dish, place pears stalk ends towards the centre. Cover with greaseproof paper and microwave on full power turning pears over half-way through. When the pears are nearly cooked, transfer them to individual serving dishes standing them upright. To thicken the sauce, blend a rounded tablespoon of corn-

flour with 4 tablespoons cold water, wine or fresh orange juice. Microwave on full power stirring frequently until the sauce thickens and is clear. Spoon over the pears. *Possible timing* 1¼ minutes per pear.

Pitted fruits (peaches and apricots)

To thaw: partly thaw in the microwave to maintain the structure and texture. Cover with greaseproof paper and microwave on low, gently repositioning the fruit, sides to middle, as soon as this is possible. Cover tightly with cling film and leave at room temperature to complete thawing. Allow 6 minutes per 500 g (1 lb) followed by a standing time of up to 20 minutes. Fruit frozen in syrup will take 3 to 4 minutes longer.

To cook: when cooking fruit whole, microwave on low. To cook halved, pitted fruit, when the shape of the finished fruit is less important, microwave on full power. Whole fruit must be scored or thoroughly pricked. *Possible timing* 2½ minutes per peach on low. Apricots – 4 minutes on full power, 8 minutes per 500 g (1 lb) on low.

Plums and greengages

To thaw: place in a shallow dish and cover with greaseproof paper. Microwave on low, gently repositioning the fruit from the sides to the middle. Allow 8 minutes per 500 g (1 lb) plus a standing time of 10 minutes. Fruit frozen in syrup should be thawed ice side up.

To cook: plums and greengages can be cooked from frozen without prior thawing. The colour of cooked fresh fruit is brighter and clearer. If desired add food colouring to the frozen variety. Cover fresh plums or greengages to avoid spattering as the skins split. Microwave on full power, stirring occasionally.

To stew: cook for three-quarters of the given time before adding sugar. Add a few tablespoons of water to each 500 g (1 lb) of plums. *Possible timing* 500 g (1 lb) – 10 minutes.

Raspberries, loganberries, boysenberries, strawberries

To thaw: treat very gently or fruit will become mushy. Remove fruit from wrapping and place in a shallow dish. Allow 6 minutes per 500 g (1 lb) on low. Gently stir from sides to middle 2 or 3 times during defrosting, preferably using a plastic spatula. When fruit is half-thawed, stir once more, then cover tightly with foil and leave to complete thawing at room temperature.

To cook: frozen fruit can be cooked without prior thawing. Fresh soft fruits are not normally cooked.

Rhubarb

To thaw: rhubarb, whether frozen cooked or raw, can be thawed on full power. Three-quarters cover with cling film and stir 2 or 3 times during defrosting. Allow 4 minutes per 500g (1 lb).

To cook: it is best to cook rhubarb fully before adding any topping. It is most important to put it in a deep dish as rhubarb tends to boil over. Three-quarters cover and stir occasionally, particularly if you see the mixture rising round the sides. Rhubarb tends to cook unevenly until the structure is broken down. Add sugar half-way through cooking. Only a few tablespoons of water are necessary as rhubarb has a high water content. *Possible timing* 5 minutes per 500g (1 lb) on full power.

Jams and preserves

Chutney

To cook: use a large heatproof bowl and microwave on high, stirring frequently. High sugar content chutney will darken and burn. Cook three-quarters covered with cling film to prevent spattering. Only half-fill the bowl with mixture. Up to 3kg (6lb) can be made at one time. Use oven gloves to protect hands. Adapt your own favourite recipes. *Possible timing* 15 minutes after mixture is soft.

Curds

To thaw: can be stored in the freezer and thawed at room temperature, but the curd will be softer than if stored in the refrigerator.

To cook: orange curd, lemon curd, grapefruit curd, lime curd are quick and simple to prepare. Use any conventional recipe or your favourite microwave recipe substituting the fruit you prefer. Combine the ingredients in large bowl. Microwave on full power stirring frequently, or on low power stirring only occasionally until mixture thickens. When a fork drawn through the mixture leaves a trail, the curd is ready. Continue beating as curd cools. *Possible timing* For 500g (1lb) — 5 minutes on full power, 12 minutes on low.

Jam
Using dried fruit
To cook: roughly chop dried fruit (e.g. apricots) and place in a large bowl. Add 2 tablespoons water for each 25g (1oz/3 tablespoons) dried fruit. Cover with cling film and microwave on full power allowing 1 minute per 25g (1oz/3 tablespoons) of fruit. Add sugar and any other ingredients when fruit is tender. *Possible timing* 15 to 20 minutes after boiling point is reached. Stir occasionally during cooking.

Using fresh and frozen fruit
Choose fruits that are high in pectin or add liquid pectin to low-rated fruits. Whether cooking from frozen or fresh, timings are similar. Do not add sugar until fruit is soft. Cook partially covered. For a thicker gel, microwave on low. This also helps to keep the shape of the fruit. After sugar has been added, always microwave on full power, stirring only

as often as is necessary to combine the boiling areas round the edge with the cooler centre. Pierce gooseberries to draw out pectin. Blackcurrants, redcurrants, apples and plums are high in pectin. Blackberries, cherries, raspberries and strawberries are low in pectin. Add 1 chopped cooking apple, a little lemon juice or commercial pectin for these fruits. For short-term storage, prepare jam jars by bringing 2.5 cm (1 in) water to the boil in them in the microwave oven. Remove with oven gloves. Pot fruit to within 2 cm (¾ in) of the rim, cover loosely with cling film, then cook each jar for 20 to 60 seconds until the cling film balloons up. Switch off immediately. This method of potting requires practice. For long-term storage, pot in the conventional way. Cling film too tightly stretched will burst. Suitable for up to 2.3 kg (5 lb) at a time. Retains colour, shape and flavour of fruit. *Possible timing* As above.

Marmalade
To cook: to draw out the pectin, the pith and pips must be cooked slowly or soaked for a long time. For successful

Use your own recipes and the general instructions provided to make your favourite jams and preserves.

marmalade in the microwave oven, chop the pips and pith finely and allow them to boil freely in the given water for 10 to 12 minutes on full power. Strain to remove the pith and pips, pressing the pulp and juice into the cooking bowl. Next add the prepared strips of peel and microwave on full power until tender. Finally add the sugar, preferably warmed, and stir until the sugar is dissolved, then microwave on full power until setting point is reached. A knob of butter will help to prevent foaming. Pot in the usual way. No more than 2.3 kg (5 lb) of preserve can be made at any one time in the microwave oven. Use the largest possible heatproof ovenglass bowl. *Possible timing* 10 minutes after boiling point is reached.

Pie filling

To cook: to prepare your own pie fillings, stew fruit in a minimum of water and thicken with cornflour. Pie fillings reheat very quickly. When used in any recipe leave a 10-minute standing time before eating.

Meat and offal

Beef

Burgers

To thaw: stand stack on plate, microwave on full power for 30 seconds to 1 minute until burgers can be separated. If only 1 or 2 are required, remove these from the top or bottom of the pile. The remainder should still be sufficiently frozen to return to the freezer.
To cook fresh burgers: put on a plate and cover with a sheet of kitchen paper towel.
To cook burgers from frozen: turn over half-way through cooking. *Possible timing* 1 to 2 minutes per burger depending upon its size and starting temperature.

Casseroles

To thaw: cover and microwave on full power breaking down the blocks and repositioning as soon as possible so that the colder parts are towards the outside of the dish. Four servings take about 15 minutes on full power. Only cook in the microwave when all pieces are completely thawed.

To cook: trim and cut beef into 2 cm (¾ in) cubes. Do not use the toughest cuts. To tenderize, before cutting into cubes, beat with a meat cleaver, use a proprietary meat tenderizer or marinate before cooking. When using full power cook the meat in a single layer without added ingredients for a quarter of the total cooking time. Add remaining ingredients and cook covered, stirring from time to time. Casseroles are best cooked on low. When cooked on high, they will be speedy but the meat will be less tender. *Possible timing* On full power 35 minutes, medium power 1¾ hours, low power 2 hours.

Mince

To thaw: shallow rectangular block will thaw more quickly than a thick block. After removing the wrappings, place the block of mince in a dish and microwave on low, breaking up the pieces around the edges as they soften. Reposition so that the frozen pieces are to the outside. Do not worry if mince begins to turn a grey colour. Although this signifies the beginning of cooking, it matters little since cooking will in any case continue as mince should not be left to stand in between thawing and cooking.

To cook: for brown results, use a preheated browning dish. Mince will also have a good flavour if added to an ordinary dish in which onions have been micro-fried (cooked on full in a tiny quantity of oil or butter). Cook mince covered with greaseproof paper until the meat is no longer pink. When preparing mince for use in other dishes, draw off the fat as it accumulates. Do not overcook or the meat will shrink and toughen. When cooking is to continue with other ingredients (e.g. chilli con carne) cook on full power for one-half the total time. Pour off surplus fat, add remaining ingredients and continue cooking for the required time. *Possible timing* Allow 8 minutes per 500 g (1 lb) on full power.

Mincemeat balls

Cook as above.

Roast beef

To thaw: do not overthaw in the microwave oven or the edges will start to cook. It is best to partially thaw by microwave. Place the joint on a rack or upturned, undecorated saucer in a shallow dish and microwave on low power allowing 9 minutes per 500 g (1 lb). Turn the joint over half-way through defrosting. Allow a standing time of 10 minutes to equalize the temperature. There will be some leeching of the juices. Save these for gravy.

To cook: cook in an unsealed roaster bag or on a roasting rack in a large shallow dish. Remove fat as it accumulates in the base. Turn the joint over and rotate the dish through 90° 4 times during cooking. Choose top-quality beef. Boned and rolled rump and topside are ideal. Choose evenly shaped joints. Allow a 10-minute standing time, tenting the joint with foil after removal from the oven and before serving. For added colour, either brush the joint with a proprietary product, gravy browning or quickly brown under the grill.

	On medium per 500g (1 lb)	*on full power per 500g (1 lb)*	*Temperature after standing*
Rare	11 minutes	6 minutes	60°C/140°F
Medium	13 minutes	7 minutes	70°C/160°F
Well-cooked	15 minutes	8½ minutes	75°C/170°F

Sausages

To thaw: unwrap, open out and separate sausages. A few seconds in the microwave on high should help. Sausages from a solid pack must be separated as soon as possible. Arrange sausages in a dish and cover with greaseproof paper. Allow 5 minutes per 500 g (1 lb) on low, repositioning the sausages every minute. Leave to stand for 3 to 4 minutes until fully thawed.

To cook: do not try to cook sausages straight from the freezer. Sausages do not brown in the microwave oven. It is a good idea to par-cook them and finish under a hot grill. The sausages are ready to grill when a skewer will plunge easily through the centre. Sausages cook superbly in the browning dish. Prick them all over, preheat the browning dish, adding a knob of salted butter towards the end of the preheating period. The butter will begin to sizzle and brown. Quickly add the well-thawed sausages, turning them over once. Without covering, cook on full power repositioning the sausages and turning them over half-way through cooking. Leave to stand for 3 minutes before

To brown roast meats place under a hot grill.

serving. For an even crisper finish, par-cook the sausages
on a plate in the microwave oven and then finish in the
browning dish. *Possible timing* 2 sausages – 2½ minutes

in the prepared and heated browning dish. 4 sausages – 4 minutes in the prepared and heated browning dish. Small thin sausages will take approximately half this time.

Steak

To thaw: do not attempt to fully thaw steaks in the microwave oven. If several steaks are to be defrosted at the same time, allow 4 minutes per 500 g (1 lb) on low, turning the steaks over and repositioning them once during defrosting. For a single steak, allow only 30 seconds on low followed by a rest period of 2 to 3 minutes; repeat as necessary. Tell-tale signs of cooking are greying and shrinking of the flesh around the outside edges. Steaks do not cook well from half-thawed state.

To cook: steaks only cook successfully in the browning dish. Preheat the browning dish to maximum adding a knob of salted butter towards the end of the preheating period. Quickly press the steaks on to the heated surface of the dish. The butter will seal and brown the first side of the steak quickly. Turn over almost immediately and continue cooking. The most successful steaks are those added to the browning dish when the butter is almost smoking. *Possible timing* 1 to 2 minutes for 1 steak, 2 to 3 minutes for 3 steaks, depending on how you like them.

Lamb

Chops

To thaw: put on a plate and cover with greaseproof or kitchen paper. Lamb chops are best thawed on low power. One chop will take 2 minutes on full power. If thawing more than one at the same time the total timing can be slightly reduced. Allow 5 minutes per 500 g (1 lb) on low, turning the chops over once during defrosting.

To cook: lamb chops will look grey when cooked in the microwave oven unless they are pre-sealed, cooked in the browning dish or brushed with a colourful sauce. Bottled sauce is suitable for this. The best thickness is 2 cm (¾ in). Cook in a single layer covered with greaseproof paper. Microwave on medium or low power pointing the bones towards the centre of the dish and giving the dish a turn through 90° 3 times during cooking. Allow a 5-minute standing time before serving. Season after cooking. Chops may also be cooked in the browning dish. *Possible timing* Allow 5-6 minutes per chop on medium or 7 to 8 minutes per chop on low. Using the preheated browning dish, cook on full power for 1½ minutes then reduce to medium or low for a further 1½ to 2 minutes.

Roast lamb

To thaw: a 1.5 kg (3½ lb) joint takes about 24 minutes on low. Allow 10 minutes per 500 g (1 lb) turning the joint over once during defrosting. Shield the thin end of the leg with smooth foil well secured and away from the oven walls as soon as this part feels even slightly warm.

To cook: lamb on the bone may cook less evenly than boned joints. For the first half of the cooking time, place the joint with the fatty side down on a rack in the dish, then turn the joint over for the remaining cooking time. Cook covered with greaseproof paper, shield any thin ends with foil which is well smoothed down as soon as this part is cooked. Make sure the foil does not touch the sides of the oven. Do not season before cooking. *Possible timing* On bone – 11 minutes per 500 g (1 lb) on medium or 8 minutes on full power. Without bone – 13 minutes per 500 g (1 lb) on medium power or 10 minutes per 500 g (1 lb) on full power. The internal temperature after standing should read 80°C/176°F.

Offal

Hearts

To thaw: arrange in a dish with the wider part towards the outside. Cover with greaseproof paper, turn over half-way through defrosting. Allow 5 minutes per 500 g (1 lb) on low power, followed by a standing time of 15 minutes.

To cook: hearts are only suitable for gentle cooking. *Possible timing* Allow 40 to 50 minutes per 500 g (1 lb) on low power.

Kidney

To thaw: spread out in a single layer on a dish lined with kitchen paper. Cover with kitchen paper and microwave on low, allowing 8 minutes per 500 g (1 lb). Turn over half-way

through defrosting. Allow a standing time.
To cook: kidneys can be gently sautéed or used with other
ingredients.

Recipe: Kidneys in Red Wine

Cut 250 g (8 oz) cleaned and cored kidneys into pieces and
toss in seasoned flour. Put into a shallow dish containing 1
tablespoon cooking oil with 1 sliced onion. Cover with
greaseproof paper and microwave on full power for 5
minutes stirring frequently. Add 3 tablespoons red wine
and 3 tablespoons water and mix well. Re-cover and
microwave on full power for 8 to 10 minutes until cooked.
Kidney and liver particularly must be covered during cooking as the skin tends to pop. *Possible timing* 500 g (1 lb) cut
up – 8 minutes on full power. Stir frequently.

Liver

To thaw: as above but reposition the pieces 3 to 4 times during defrosting.

To cook: chicken livers should be roughly chopped or halved before cooking. Liver should only be cooked until it is just pink inside. Overcooking will cause toughening.

Possible timing 6 to 8 minutes per 500 g (1 lb) on full power.

LEFT: Kidneys in Red Wine. ABOVE: Chicken Liver Pâté.

Recipe: Chicken Liver Pâté

Place 50 g (2 oz/4 tablespoons) butter and 1 chopped onion in a large shallow dish. Microwave on full power for 2 minutes. Stir in 250 g (8 oz) chopped chicken livers and 1 teaspoon mixed herbs. Cover with greaseproof paper and microwave on full power for 7 minutes or until livers are cooked. Blend to a purée in a liquidizer with 75 g (3 oz/6 tablespoons) butter. Stir in 1 tablespoon sherry, 1 teaspoon mustard powder, salt and freshly ground black pepper to taste. Chill before serving.

Tongue

To thaw: tongue is dense and is difficult to defrost in one stage. Transfer it to the refrigerator for a few hours to commence the thawing. To complete thawing, curve the tongue round the inside edges of a large shallow dish. Microwave on low power for 4 minutes per 500g (1 lb). Allow a standing time of 30 minutes. Repeat as necessary. Turn the dish 3 times through 90° during the defrosting period and tent in foil during the standing time. Small tongue such as lamb's tongue may be thawed directly from the freezer, allowing 10 minutes per 500g (1 lb) on low, followed by a 15-minute standing time.

To cook: soak the tongue in cold water for 6 hours. Drain and put in a large casserole with a little chopped onion, chopped carrot and a bouquet garni. Cover with boiling water. Cover with cling film or a lid and cook on full power giving the dish a 90° turn 4 times during cooking. Drain and skin while hot. Serve hot or cold. *Possible timing* 20 minutes per 500g (1 lb) on full power when covered with boiling water.

Tripe

To thaw: thaw small quantities in the microwave on low power allowing 10 minutes per 500g (1 lb), followed by a 15-minute standing time.

To cook: tripe may be cooked in the microwave oven on low power but little time will be saved. When cooked in a large amount of water, the oven cavity may run with water due to the condensation. However, it is useful to parboil by microwave followed by further cooking in the pressure cooker, slow cooker or saucepan. Place tripe in a deep dish in cold salted water, seven-eighths cover with cling film and microwave on full power for 10 minutes, then proceed according to your favourite recipe.

Pork

Bacon

To thaw: to separate slices, place in original plastic wrapping on oven shelf and microwave on full power for 15 seconds. Leave to stand for 5 minutes. To thaw a complete pack of bacon, microwave on low power for 1 or 2 minutes.

To cook: cook covered to prevent spattering. For large quantities cook on a microwave rack in a dish, covering with kitchen paper to absorb splashing. Microwave on full power, overlapping lean and fat. Crispy bacon can be cooked in the browning dish. Times vary so watch carefully, rashers can become hard. *Possible timing* 1 rasher, 30 seconds to 1 minute. Allow 12 to 14 minutes per 500 g (1 lb) depending upon thickness of rashers and the way they are arranged in the dish.

Bacon joint

To thaw: place the pouch on a plate in the microwave oven and slit the top. Microwave on low, only until the outside feels just warm. Allow 8 minutes per 500 g (1 lb). Leave to stand for 30 minutes to complete thawing. If after this time thawing is not complete, repeat the process.

To cook: bacon joints cook well in a roaster bag sealed loosely with string. Place the bag in a shallow dish. It is best to cook on half power and if the joint is large, it should be turned over half-way through the cooking period. A probe is useful when cooking bacon or ham and this should be inserted into the centre of the joint during cooking. Pre-cooked ham should be reheated to 50°C/122°F and raw joints to 70°C/160°F. Use a meat thermometer to test if your oven doesn't have a probe. Do not use a meat thermometer in the microwave oven unless it is one specially designed for use in the microwave. Allow 10 to 15 minutes standing time before serving. *Possible timing* Pre-cooked joints: 11 minutes per 500 g (1 lb) on medium. Raw joints: 14 minutes per 500 g (1 lb) on medium. In ovens with only full power and low settings, microwave at full power for 5 minutes per 500 g (1 lb) then reduce to low power for 10 minutes per 500 g (1 lb).

Chops

To thaw: put chops on a plate with the thinner parts towards the middle. Cover with greaseproof paper and microwave on low allowing 8½ minutes per 500 g (1 lb). Leave to stand for 5 minutes before continuing to cook.

To cook: arrange in the dish with the thinner parts towards the middle. Cover with greaseproof paper, turn the dish through 90° 3 times during cooking. Cook until the flesh is no longer pink inside and leave to stand for at least 3 minutes before serving. The chops should be covered during this time. Always serve on heated plates as chops lose their heat quickly. Pork chops are very successful when cooked in the microwave. Brown well in a browning dish. *Possible timing* Allow 4 to 4½ minutes per average chop.

Fillet
Thaw and cook as veal escalope (see page 67).

Gammon
Thaw as bacon joint (see page 65).
To cook: slash through fat at 2.5 cm (1 in) intervals to prevent meat curling up as it shrinks. Cover and microwave on full power, turning steaks over half-way through cooking. Baste 3 or 4 times during cooking to prevent drying out. *Possible timing* 250 g (8 oz) steak, 3 minutes on full power.

Ham joint
Thaw and cook as bacon joint (see page 65).

Ham, sliced and cooked
To thaw: for a 125 g (4 oz) pack of sliced, cooked ham, allow 3 minutes on low power and leave to stand 5 minutes. Turn pack over once during thawing.

Ham roast
To thaw: defrost on low power allowing 8½ minutes per 500 g (1 lb). Turn joint over half-way and also turn the dish

through 90° 3 times during the defrosting time. After the given time remove from the microwave oven and tent with foil for the temperature to equalize. Choose even-shaped joints. Allow to stand for 30 minutes if not defrosted. Remember defrosting time is influenced by the size, shape and the starting temperature of the joint.

To cook: slash the skin in several places and sprinkle liberally with salt. Place on a trivet or upturned undecorated saucer in a dish and microwave on medium until the temperature reaches 75°C/170°F. Allow a standing time of 20 minutes. It is essential that pork is completely cooked. Alternatively, cook on full power. *Possible timing* On medium power 11 to 15 minutes per 500g (1 lb) or on full power 9 to 10 minutes.

Sausages
Thaw and cook as beef sausages (see page 58).

Veal
Chops
Thaw and cook as lamb chops (see page 60).

Escalopes
To thaw: because escalopes are beaten thinly and the diameter is large, thawing in the microwave oven may not be suitable. However, it is possible to partly thaw on low for

30 seconds and complete thawing under cold running water.

To cook: dip the escalopes in beaten egg and golden crumbs. Put a tablespoon of cooking oil in a round dish and microwave covered on full power for 1 minute. Add the veal escalopes and microwave on full power for 30 to 45 seconds, then turn the escalopes over and cook for a further 30 seconds. Transfer to a warm serving dish and cover with foil while remaining escalopes are cooking. Escalopes can also be cooked without crumbs or in a preheated, buttered browning dish. *Possible timing* 2 minutes per escalope depending on the size. Do not over-cook. To test, make an incision in the centre. The flesh should be just opaque.

Roast veal

To thaw: thaw gently in the refrigerator or microwave on low in a dish covered with greaseproof paper, allowing 3 minutes per 500 g (1 lb) followed by a 30-minute resting time, repeat as necessary.

To cook: cook in a roasting bag to prevent drying out. Do not seal the bag. It is best to cook on medium power but veal can be roasted on full power. The temperature after a 15-minute standing time should read 75°C/170°F. *Possible timing* 11 minutes per 500 g (1 lb) on half power or 9 minutes on full power.

Pastry

Choux

To thaw: defrosting of baked choux pastry depends on filling. Because by nature it is light and airy, empty shells will quickly collapse if defrosted in the microwave oven. Microwave filled buns on full power for 20 seconds, then leave to stand at room temperature. For small unfilled buns arrange in a circle on the oven shelf and microwave on low for 30 seconds.

To cook: choux dough can be prepared in the microwave but can only be cooked successfully in the traditional manner. During cooking the pastry will rise and set, de-veloping a texture similar to a starch-reduced roll. Put the butter in the water and bring to the boil in a bowl on full power in the microwave oven, then stir in the flour. *Possible timing* 25 g (1 oz/2 tablespoons) butter plus 5 tablespoons water takes 1½ minutes.

Pies and flans
To thaw: no specific recommendations can be made since the filling is the determining factor. Usually it is better to thaw on a low setting. The centre must be allowed to catch up with the outer edges.

Puff
To thaw: remove pastry wrapping and place on a sheet of greaseproof paper on the oven shelf. Microwave for 20 seconds on full power, turning the pastry through 90° half-way through defrosting. Leave to stand at room temperature for a minimum of 10 minutes. Pastry should be firm and cool when rolling out.
To cook: after rolling out and trimming, refrigerate the pastry before using. Do not chill in the freezer. Microwave on full power until the pastry is fully risen and does not flop when the door is opened. Watch carefully as puff pastry quickly burns inside. Does not brown on the outside. *Possible timing* 2½ minutes per 200 g (7 oz) oblong rolled to 3 mm (⅛ in) thick on full power.

Shortcrust
To thaw: when preparing home-made shortcrust for the freezer, shape into an even block rather than a ball. Remove wrappings and place on the oven shelf. Microwave on full power for ½ minute for a small pack and 45 seconds for a large pack. Turn the pastry through 90° half-way through defrosting. Leave the pastry to stand at room temperature until pliable enough to roll.
To cook: roll out and fit the pastry into a dish which should be no more than 23 cm (9 in) in diameter. Prick the base. Bake blind in the microwave oven using baking beans on kitchen paper. Microwave on full power. Remove the paper and beans as soon as the pastry is set, then continue cooking as necessary. The pastry is ready when the appearance is opaque and flaky bubbles appear on the surface. This pastry is best in quiches. *Possible timing* An average pastry case takes 4 to 5 minutes.

Poultry and game

Chicken
Casserole
To thaw: if the casserole has been frozen in a suitable dish, place this in the microwave oven and three-quarters cover with cling film. Blocks of casserole should be turned into a suitable dish ice side up and covered with greaseproof paper. Microwave on full power stirring and repositioning the pieces frequently. Break up blocks as soon as they give. For the most even results, place a small bowl or glass in the centre. This will keep the food towards the outside of the dish. A large casserole will take up to 15 minutes on full power.

To cook: casseroles containing large amounts of liquid may be microwaved on full power. Casseroles using a small amount of gravy or sauce should be microwaved on low. Best results are obtained by using a medium amount of liquid and microwave on medium. *Possible timing* 30 to 40 minutes on medium power for a cut-up 1.5 kg (3½ lb) bird plus other ingredients.

Portions
To thaw: arrange pieces on a plate with the thinner part towards the middle. Cover and microwave on low, turning the pieces over once during defrosting. Turn the dish through 90° 3 times during defrosting. Take great care – the thinner parts, particularly drum sticks, can begin to cook. Allow 7 minutes per 500 g (1 lb).

To cook: chicken must be fully thawed before cooking. Microwave on full power until the juices near the bone run clear. Place bone ends of drumsticks towards the centre of the dish. Cook covered with greaseproof paper as the skin may spatter. *Possible timing* 2½ to 3½ minutes for 1 piece. 6 to 9 minutes per 4 pieces. Allow a standing time of 10 to 15 minutes for thicker pieces.

Roast chicken
To thaw: must be completely thawed before cooking. Remove the wrappings and put the chicken in a dish. It is best to thaw on low power allowing 6 minutes per 500 g

(1 lb). Turn the chicken over and rotate the dish through 90° 4 times during the defrosting period. Remove the giblets as soon as the bag can be loosened. Complete defrosting by running under the cold tap or immersing the bird in cold water until all ice crystals have melted.

To cook: rub the chicken with softened butter and paprika. Season inside the cavity. Cover loosely during cooking, turning the chicken over so that it cooks equally on all 4 sides and turning the dish through 90° 4 times during cooking. Test twice with a thermometer which should not touch the bone or float inside the empty cavity. When the thermometer registers 82°C/180°F, tent with foil and leave

Roast chicken may be browned under the grill.

to stand for 15 minutes until the temperature reaches 90°C/195°F. During cooking tuck wing tips and ends of legs close to the carcase. Small pieces of aluminium foil can be used to cover the tips of wings and legs to prevent them becoming overcooked and burnt. This foil must not touch the sides of the microwave oven. *Possible timing* 9 minutes per 500 g (1 lb) on medium power or 6 minutes on full power.

Duck
To thaw: thaw as for chicken (see above). An average duck takes 30 to 40 minutes plus an equal standing time. It is best to commence thawing in the refrigerator.
To cook: duck is very fatty so should be placed on a trivet or upturned saucer in the dish. The fat should be spooned away as soon as it accumulates. Cover with greaseproof paper to prevent spattering or cook in a roaster bag. Turn over and turn round 4 times during cooking. Microwave on medium power or on full power. *Possible timing* 10 minutes per 500 g (1 lb) on medium power, 7 minutes on full power. Temperature after 15 minutes standing time 90°C/195°F.

Goose
To thaw: remove from wrappings and place in a shallow dish. Microwave on low power turning the bird over every 10 minutes. Allow 5 minutes per 500 g (1 lb). An average goose weighing 4 kg (9 lb) takes approximately 45 minutes. Leave to stand for 1 hour before cooking. Rinse under the cold tap to remove any ice crystals.
To cook: Goose must not be cooked with the giblets in the cavity and it is best to remove as much fat as possible. Prepare in the usual way and stuff if desired. Use wooden cocktail sticks or string to secure the legs and wings. Place breast-side up on a trivet or saucer in a shallow dish, cover with greaseproof paper or cook in a roaster bag. Microwave on full power until thermometer reads 75°C/175°F. Turn goose over and turn dish through 90° every 15 minutes during cooking. Tent with foil and leave to stand for at least 15 minutes after removal from the microwave oven. Brown under a hot grill if desired. *Possible timing* Average-sized goose − 1 to 1¼ hours.

Rabbit

To thaw: arrange pieces on a dish with the thinner parts towards the inside or overlapping. Cover and microwave on low power allowing 11 minutes per 500g (1 lb). Reposition and stir frequently during defrosting and leave a standing time of 10 minutes before cooking. Blocks of rabbit pieces: place block ice side up in dish and separate as soon as thawing commences, moving the colder pieces to the centre.

To cook: as for chicken casserole (see page 70).

Turkey

To thaw: large turkeys are difficult to thaw completely in the microwave oven. It is best to slow thaw in the refrigerator; a very large turkey will take 3 days. You can use the microwave oven to complete thawing. Treat as for chicken remembering to remove the giblets as soon as possible and cover the wing tips and legs with foil as soon as they are thawed, making sure that the foil does not touch the sides of the oven. After thawing, run under cold water to remove remaining ice crystals.

To cook: prepare in the traditional way. Before cooking dry the surface with kitchen paper and rub with butter or browning mixture. Place the entire dish in a roaster bag, leaving it unsealed, and cook preferably on medium power. Shield the breast and wing tips with aluminium foil as soon as they are cooked being careful that the foil does not touch the sides of the oven. A large turkey may take 2 to 3 hours to cook. Tent with foil during a minimum standing time of 20 minutes. For best results, complete cooking in a conventional oven. Birds over 8 kg (18 lb) are unsuitable for microwave cooking. *Possible timing* 11 to 13 minutes per 500g (1 lb) on medium or 9 to 11 minutes on full power. Internal temperature after standing time should be 90°C/195°F.

Venison

To thaw: thaw on a dish in the microwave oven allowing 10 minutes per 500g (1 lb) on low power. To prevent the possibility of the joint cooking on the outside, allow a standing time of 15 minutes half-way through defrosting. Leave to stand tented for 45 minutes until fully thawed.

Venison can also be thawed using full power. Allow 1 minute per 500 g (1 lb) followed by a standing time of 10 minutes, then repeat as necessary.

To cook: venison cutlets cook well by microwave provided the meat is from a young animal. Tough cuts must be tenderized prior to cooking. Brown in a preheated and well-buttered browning dish, then add a few tablespoons of whisky or brandy, cranberry sauce and orange juice. Cover with the lid and cook on full power turning the dish through 90° 4 times during cooking. *Possible timing* 4 cutlets – 15 minutes. *Possible timing* On ovens with no medium setting, double the given cooking times and microwave on low.

Puddings and desserts

Baked custards

To thaw: large cooked custards should not be frozen but individual custards may be thawed on low power although good results cannot be guaranteed. Unbaked custards freeze well. Microwave on low power stirring as soon as it is possible to do so. Continue gentle stirring until the mixture

is just warm. Thawing and cooking can be carried out in one continuous process.

To cook: egg custards come under the 'critical' category and should be cooked on low power. Can also be cooked on full power provided a container of water is also placed in the oven. When a large volume is to be cooked in one dish, warm milk first. *Possible timing* 600 ml (1 pt/2½ cups) baked custard mixture containing 600 ml (1 pt/2½ cups) milk and 4 eggs, 10-14 minutes on low power.

Crumbles

To thaw: crumbles are very versatile. Crumble may be used straight from the freezer. Defrost crumble-topped dishes on low power. To test, feel both the top and the underside of the dish, which should not feel frozen.

To cook: cook fruit crumbles in a deep dish. It is best to thaw frozen fruit before adding topping. Allow 250 g (8 oz) crumble mix to 500 g (1 lb) fruit, adding sugar only if fruit has not been cooked prior to freezing. Microwave on full

Sponge puddings are successful in the microwave; meringue toppings can be browned under the grill.

power allowing extra time if fruit has not previously been thawed. Allow a 5-minute standing time before browning or serving. Turn the dish through 90° 3 times during the cooking process. *Possible timing* 12 to 15 minutes per 500g (1 lb) combined weight of crumble mix and fruit on full power.

Milk puddings

To thaw: thaw on full power, stirring as soon as possible. Add 2 or 3 tablespoons fresh cold milk half-way through thawing. An average rice pudding takes 12 minutes. It is best to use homogenized or skimmed milk when preparing milk puddings for the freezer.

To cook: cook on medium power or low power as soon as the liquid is hot. When cooked on full power milk tends to boil over. Use a tall bowl. Cook rice in water first on full power. *Possible timing* 25 to 30 minutes on low power after rice is swollen or 6 minutes on full power after rice is cooked.

Tapioca

To cook: cook as for rice but reduce the cooking time in water.

Semolina and Sago

To cook: must only be cooked on a low setting.

Sponge pudding

To thaw: thaw and heat in one stage. Sponge puddings must not be thawed in a tin or foil container. Place in pudding basin or serving dish. Cover loosely with cling film and microwave on full power for 4 minutes per 500g (1 lb) pudding. Leave to stand for 4 minutes before serving as jam, syrup and treacle become very hot indeed.

To cook: prepare according to your favourite recipe but add 1 teaspoon golden syrup and one extra tablespoon liquid. Only half-fill the pudding basin and if using jam or similar syrup in the base, the pudding basin must be resistant to extremely high temperatures. Cover loosely with cling film to enable the pudding to rise. Cook on full power until the pudding is just dry on top. Remove cling film carefully and allow a standing time of 5 minutes before serving. Pudding basins must be greased. *Possible timing* 4 minutes on full power.

Rice, pasta and pulses

Beans, kidney
To reheat: do not cook kidney beans in the microwave oven as long, high temperature cooking is required. However, it is possible to reheat kidney beans. Drain, place in a dish and cover with cling film. Microwave on full or medium power. *Possible timing* 3 to 4 minutes per large can.

Lasagne
To thaw: lasagne is slow to thaw and reheat. Microwave at full power for 5 minutes followed by a 5-minute resting period. Repeat as necessary. Four servings may take as long as 25 minutes to reheat from frozen.
To cook: put boiling salted water in a large casserole to which has been added a teaspoon of cooking oil. Bring back to the boil on full power, then add 1 or 2 sheets of pasta. Bring back to the boil once more, then add the remaining pasta. Eight sheets of pasta require 1 l (1¾ pt/ 4¼ cups) boiling water and 1 teaspoon each of salt and oil. It is best to use quick-cooking pasta. *Possible timing* Cook on full power for 6 minutes, then cover and leave to stand 10 minutes before draining.

Lentils and split peas
To thaw: place block of pre-cooked, frozen pulse dishes in a tall, narrow container. Three-quarters cover with cling film, microwave on full power, stirring frequently.
To cook: it is best to pre-soak as this reduces cooking time by half. Split peas take a little longer than lentils, which are smaller. Cook in a deep container to prevent boiling over. Start cooking at full power, then reduce to low power half-way through cooking. Stir frequently. Only lentils can be cooked without pre-soaking. After rinsing stir in plenty of boiling water. Add salt after cooking. *Possible timing* Microwave on full power without covering for 20 minutes or 10 minutes on full power followed by 25 minutes on low power. Overcooking is not a problem provided extra water is added if necessary.

Macaroni and small pasta shapes

To thaw: it will take as long to thaw and reheat a pasta dish as it would to cook the pasta freshly in the microwave oven. If the pasta is frozen in a sauce, arrange the pasta round the outside of the dish and the sauce in the middle and cover with cling film. In dishes such as macaroni cheese, stir in a few tablespoons of warmed milk as soon as the pasta begins to thaw out. When possible separate into lumps and stir during cooking. Thaw on full power unless the dish cannot be stirred. Then thaw on low power.

To cook: up to 250g (8oz/2cups) can be satisfactorily cooked in the microwave oven on full power. Put the pasta in a large deep dish, adding 1l (1¾pt/4¼cups) boiling water and 1 teaspoon each of oil and salt. Stir thoroughly.

Possible timing Allow 6 minutes on full power, then cover and leave to stand for 8 to 10 minutes.

Rice, spaghetti and lentils.

Pearl barley

To cook: cook pearl barley in a large covered dish in plenty of boiling water. As the barley swells, it may be necessary to add more water. Stir frequently. *Possible timing* 30 to 45 minutes.

Ravioli

To cook: ravioli filled with meat cooks more quickly than ravioli filled with cheese, so allow a little longer for the latter. Put 1.5 l (2½ pt/6¼ cups) boiling water in a very large casserole and stir in ½ teaspoon salt. Bring back to the boil on full power in the microwave oven, then add the pasta a few pieces at a time and stir briskly. Bring back to the boil and when bubbling, add the remaining pasta. Microwave on full power, then cover. The maximum amount that can be cooked at one time is 250 g (8 oz); it should be cooked in plenty of water to prevent sticking. *Possible timing* 6 to 8 minutes, standing time 10 to 12 minutes.

Rice

To thaw: turn the block upside down in the serving dish. Without covering, microwave large quantities on low and small quantities on full power. Break up the lumps as soon as it is possible and stir the rice occasionally during thawing. Continue reheating if required adding an extra 2 to 3 minutes on full power. As a rough guide, 350 g (12 oz/

Type of rice	Quantity
Long grain rice (traditional method)	50 g (2 oz/4 tbsp)
	125 g (4 oz/8 tbsp)
	250 g (8 oz/1¼ cups)
Long grain rice (all-in-one method)	50 g (2 oz/4 tbsp)
	125 g (4 oz/8 tbsp)
	250 g (8 oz/1¼ cups)
Brown rice	125 g (4 oz/8 tbsp)

Spaghetti

To thaw: for large quantities of spaghetti it is easier and quicker to reheat in a pan of boiling water. For up to 250 g (8 oz) cooked spaghetti, thaw on low power. Allow about 10 minutes. The frozen spaghetti must be covered and stirred frequently, separating the strands with a fork. Where spaghetti is frozen with a sauce, it is best to mix the sauce together with the spaghetti before freezing. When the sauce and spaghetti are separated, try to arrange the pasta around the outside of the dish and the sauce in the middle. When freezing spaghetti without the sauce, arrange in a ring before freezing.

To cook: cook in small quantities, about 125 g (4 oz) at once. Two-thirds fill a deep casserole with about 600 ml (1 pt/2½ cups) boiling water. Bring back to the boil in the microwave oven, stir in 1 teaspoon oil and ½ teaspoon salt and quickly swirl in the spaghetti. Without covering, micro-wave on full power. Ensure that no pieces of spaghetti protrude over the edge of the dish as these will remain hard. *Possible timing* 6 minutes, then cover and leave to stand 10 minutes before draining.

2 cups) of cooked rice will take 12 minutes on low power or 5 minutes on full power. When reheating cold rice, first add 2 teaspoons cold water. Frozen rice needs no extra liquid. *To cook:* follow instructions for conventional boiling, but allow a little extra water and use the chart (see below) as a guide. Use a large casserole dish as the rice will swell to three times its dry volume. Microwave on full power.

Boiling water	Salt	Cooking time (minutes)
300 ml (½ pt/1¼ cups)	½ tsp	8
450 ml (¾ pt/2 cups)	1 tsp	10
600 ml (1 pt/2½ cups)	1½ tsp	12
150 ml (¼ pt/⅔ cup)	¼ tsp	6
300 ml (½ pt/1¼ cups)	½ tsp	10
600 ml (1 pt/2½ cups)	1 tsp	15
450 ml (¾ pt/2 cups)	½ tsp	20

Sauces

Basic roux

To thaw: thaw in a bowl, allowing 10 minutes on low or 4 minutes on full power for 600 ml (1 pt/2½ cups) sauce. Cover during thawing but stir as soon as it is possible. Continue stirring every 15 to 20 seconds and as soon as the sauce is thawed, beat thoroughly with a whisk.

To cook: use your favourite recipe but cook in the microwave oven in a large bowl 2½ times the volume of the liquid. This is to allow for boiling up. Put the butter in the bowl and microwave on full power until just melted. Stir in the flour and cook for 30 seconds to 1 minute until the mixture puffs up. Add the liquid using a whisk to mix. Continue microwaving on full power, whisking once after the liquid is warm, then twice more during cooking. Whisk again before serving. The thicker the sauce, the quicker it will cook. Sauces cook well in the microwave as there are no lumps; they can be cooked in advance and later reheated. *Possible timing* 300 ml (½ pt/1¼ cups) – 3 minutes, 600 ml (1 pt/2½ cups) – 5 minutes, 1.2 l (2 pt/5 cups) – 6 minutes for a pouring or coating consistency.

Adapt your favourite sauce recipes by following the general instructions provided.

Egg custard sauce

To cook: use 2 egg yolks to 300 ml (½ pt/1¼ cups) milk. Beat together thoroughly and microwave on full power for 30 seconds. Then continue cooking on low power. Whisk every 30 seconds. *Possible timing* 300 ml (½ pt/1¼ cups) – 5 minutes.

Cornflour or packet custard sauce

To cook: blend the powder with a little of the cold measured milk in a large bowl. Add remaining milk. Microwave on full power, whisking 3 times during cooking. *Possible timing* 300 ml (½ pt/1¼ cups) takes 2½ minutes.

Emulsified sauces

To thaw: 600 ml (1 pt/2½ cups) sauce takes 6 minutes on low or 2 minutes on full power. Only use full power if you are completely confident as overheating causes curdling. Microwave uncovered and stir frequently.

To cook: Hollandaise and similar sauces: microwave on medium power or with great care on full power. Melt the butter in a large bowl in the microwave oven, then add the eggs which should be previously beaten with any other ingredients. Pour the blended eggs into the melted butter and microwave, whisking frequently and vigorously. Continue beating as the sauce cools. Emulsified sauces may be reheated but this must only be on the lowest possible setting. *Possible timing* 1 minute on full power, 3 minutes on low power.

Fruit sauce (arrowroot)

To thaw: thaw in a narrow container on full power beating frequently. Press through a sieve if lumps remain.

Raspberry jam sauce is a delicious topping for ice cream.

To cook: allow 2 level teaspoons to 300 ml (½ pt/1¼ cups) liquid. Blend the arrowroot with a little of the cold liquid, then add the remainder. Microwave on full power, whisking 2 to 3 times during cooking. Sauce is ready when colour clears. *Possible timing* 3 minutes for 300 ml (½ pt/1¼ cups) on full power.

Gravy

To cook: if roasting dish is suitable for the microwave, cook gravy in this. Otherwise transfer drippings from roast into suitable ovenproof glass bowl. Stir in flour or gravy powder and stock. Microwave on full power whisking occasionally. *Possible timing* 3½ minutes per 300 ml (½ pt/1¼ cups).

Jam sauce

To cook: combine equal quantities of jam and water with a few drops of lemon juice if preferred. Microwave on full power in glass heat-resistant jug, stirring once or twice during cooking to blend. *Possible timing* 150 ml (¼ pt/⅔ cup) takes 1½ minutes. Do not overcook or sauce will revert to jam.

Soups

Canned

To heat: pour soup into bowl. Three-quarters cover, microwave on full power, stirring twice during reheating. Soup must be well mixed before tasting. *Possible timing* 1 × 285 g (10½ oz) can – 3 to 3½ minutes on full power.

Creamed

To thaw: put block in bowl. Microwave on full power, three-quarters covered. Break down the block as soon as it is possible and turn it over if you can. Stir frequently. Allow 6 minutes per 600 ml (1 pt/2½ cups). If soup is to be served cold, thaw only until a few small lumps remain, then beat or stir until these dissolve.

To cook: microwave on full power. Sauté the vegetables in a large bowl in the given quantity of butter. Stir in the flour and half the liquid. Microwave on full power, beating occasionally. When the soup is thick, purée in a liquidizer or press through a sieve. Add the remaining liquid and bring back to the boil. If the liquid consists mainly of milk, make sure the bowl is large. *Possible timing* Depends on the ingredients used. Average 10 minutes.

Packet

To cook: reconstitute according to manufacturer's instructions reducing the liquid by one-fifth. Microwave on full power for thick soups and medium power for soups consisting of a mixture of liquid and solids. *Possible timing* 6 minutes for thick, 12 minutes for mixed.

Puréed

To thaw: as for creamed soups (see above).

To cook: microwave on full power in a minimum of liquid. Add remaining liquid after soup is puréed and bring back to the boil in the microwave oven. To thicken, blend cornflour with cold water. Whisk into the boiling soup. *Possible timing* Depends on vegetables used. Average 15 minutes.

Stocks

To thaw: put block in a bowl and microwave on full power allowing 7 minutes per 600 ml (1 pt/2½ cups). Break up and turn the block over as soon as it is possible. Fish stock tends to separate into liquid and jelly when thawed.

To cook: beef stock not suitable. Chicken stock: cut up carcase and place in large bowl with any skin and other bones. Cover with water and three-quarters cover the bowl with cling film. Chicken stock spatters as it boils. Microwave on full power to boiling point, then reduce to medium power or low. Small quantities of stock can be reheated in the microwave oven. Use a saucepan for large amounts. *Possible timing* 45 minutes.

Fish stock: place cut up bones and skin in a large bowl, cover with water and three-quarters cover with cling film. Microwave on full power until boiling, then reduce to low power. Stir occasionally during cooking. When cooked, strain and use as required, or cool completely and freeze.

When a large amount of stock has been frozen in one container, bring any unused thawed portion to the boil daily. *Possible timing* Not more than 15 minutes after boiling point is reached.

Guide to cooking vegetables

Fresh Vegetables

Type of Vegetable	Quantity	Water
Artichokes, globe	1 2 4	8 tbsp (½ cup) 8 tbsp (½ cup) 250 ml (8 fl oz/1 cup)
Artichokes, Jerusalem	As for Parsnips	
Asparagus	750 g (1½ lb)	8 tbsp (½ cup)
Aubergine (Eggplant)	2 medium, halved	2 tbsp
Beans, green (*except thin* French beans)	500 g (1 lb) 250 g (½ lb)	8 tbsp (½ cup) 12 tbsp (¾ cup)
Beans, broad *podded*	500 g (1 lb)	12 tbsp (¾ cup)
Beetroot	2 medium	8 tbsp (½ cup)
Broccoli	500 g (1 lb)	8 tbsp (½ cup)
Brussels sprouts	500 g (1 lb)	4 tbsp (¼ cup)
Cabbage, *quartered*	500 g (1 lb)	8 tbsp (½ cup)
Cabbage, *shredded*	500 g (1 lb)	8 tbsp (½ cup)
Carrots, *whole*	6 medium	8 tbsp (½ cup)

Salt	Cooking Time	Comments
½ tsp	5-6 mins	Turn upside down to drain before serving.
½ tsp	7-8 mins	
1 tsp	14-15 mins	
½ tsp	11-14 mins	Arrange thicker stems towards the outside. Give the dish a half-turn after 6 minutes.
–	7-9 mins	Scoop out the cooked flesh and use as required.
½ tsp	12-16 mins	Stir twice. Do not overcook.
½ tsp	8-10 mins	Stir several times. Best cooked conventionally
½ tsp	8 mins	Stir 2 or 3 times.
½ tsp	12-16 mins	Leave to stand for 10 minutes before peeling. Do not overcook.
1 tsp	10-12 mins	Cut into even-sized pieces. Stir once.
½ tsp	7-8 mins	Choose evenly shaped sprouts. Stir once.
½ tsp	10-12 mins	Rearrange once.
½ tsp	9-11 mins	Stir once.
½ tsp	10-12 mins	Thicker ends should be towards the outside. Rearrange once.

Type of Vegetable	Quantity	Water
Carrots, *sliced*	375 g (¾ lb)	8 tbsp (½ cup)
Cauliflower, *whole*	750 g (1½ lb)	8 tbsp (½ cup)
Cauliflower, *florets*	500 g (1 lb)	8 tbsp (½ cup)
Celery, *whole or sliced*	500 g (1 lb)	4 tbsp (¼ cup)
Chicory (Endive), *whole*	4 medium pieces	4 tbsp (¼ cup)
Corn-on-the-cob	1 cob 2 cobs	– 4 tbsp (¼ cup)
Courgettes (Zucchini), *topped and tailed*	8 small	–
Fennel, *cut in quarters*	500 g (1 lb)	4 tbsp (¼ cup)
Leeks, *trimmed and sliced*	500 g (1 lb)	4 tbsp (¼ cup)
Marrow (Squash), *sliced*	500 g (1 lb)	–
Mushrooms	250 g (½ lb)	2 tbsp
Okra, *topped and tailed, washed and drained*	500 g (1 lb)	8 tbsp (½ cup)
Onions	4 medium	4 tbsp (¼ cup)

Salt	Cooking Time	Comments
½ tsp	10-12 mins	Slices must be no more than 1 cm (½ in) thick.
½ tsp	12-16 mins	Cook on medium, turning over half-way through cooking. Start with stalk uppermost.
½ tsp	10-12 mins	Stir once.
¼ tsp	14-16 mins	Stir once.
–	5-8 mins	Rearrange once. Add salt after cooking.
–	3-4 mins	Cook in husk if preferred.
–	6-8 mins	
–	7 mins	Sprinkle with nutmeg and dot with butter before cooking. Rearrange once.
–	12-14 mins	Stir once.
½ tsp	10-12 mins	Stir once.
–	8-10 mins	Use greaseproof (waxed) paper to cover. Add salt after cooking.
–	2-4 mins	Do not overcook.
½ tsp	5 mins	Stir twice. Drain and braise in butter 5 minutes on low.
½ tsp	10-12 mins	Stir once. Turn large onions over half-way through cooking.

Type of Vegetable	Quantity	Water
Parsnips, *cubed*	500 g (1 lb)	10 tbsp (½ cup)
Peas, *shelled*	500 g (1 lb)	10 tbsp (½ cup)
Potatoes, *peeled and quartered*	500 g (1 lb)	10 tbsp (½ cup)
Potatoes, *softened*	500 g (1 lb)	—
Potatoes, *baked in skins*, or sweet potatoes	2 medium	—
Pumpkin, *cubed*	As for turnips	
Salsify	As for parsnips	
Spinach	500 g (1 lb)	—
Swedes, *cubed*	As for turnips	
Tomatoes, *halved*	2	—
Turnips, *cubed*	500 g (1 lb)	10 tbsp (½ cup)

Salt	Cooking Time	Comments
¼ tsp	12-14 mins	Add lemon juice before cooking. Stir once.
½ tsp	9-11 mins	Stir once.
½ tsp	10-14 mins	Stir once.
–	5 mins	Cook in unsealed roaster bag. Shake during cooking and drain carefully.
–	7-8 mins	Prick thoroughly. Cook on kitchen paper
	10-12 mins	
–	6-8 mins	Microwave in an unsealed roaster bag. Add salt after cooking.
¼ tsp	1-1½ mins	Add pepper and a knob of butter before cooking. No standing time required.
¼ tsp	14-16 mins	Stir twice. Mash after standing time.

Frozen Vegetables

Type of Vegetable	Quantity	Water
Artichoke hearts	250 g (½ lb)	2 tbsp
Asparagus tips	250 g (½ lb)	4 tbsp (¼ cup)
Beans, green (*except* thin French beans)	250 g (½ lb) 250 g (½ lb)	8 tbsp (½ cup) 12 tbsp (¾ cup)
Broccoli	250 g (½ lb)	8 tbsp (½ cup)
Brussels sprouts	250 g (½ lb)	8 tbsp (½ cup)
Cabbage, *shredded*	250 g (½ lb)	6 tbsp
Carrots, *whole or diced*	250 g (½ lb)	4 tbsp (¼ cup)
Cauliflower florets	250 g (½ lb)	–
Corn-on-the-cob	2 cobs 4 cobs	– –
Corn kernels	250 g (½ lb)	2 tbsp
Courgettes (Zucchini), *sliced*	250 g (½ lb)	–
Mushrooms	250 g (½ lb)	–
Onions, *small whole*	250 g (½ lb)	–
Peas	250 g (½ lb)	4 tbsp (¼ cup)
Peas & Carrots, *mixed*	250 g (½ lb)	2 tbsp
Peas & Onions, *mixed*	250 g (½ lb)	2 tbsp

Salt	Cooking Time	Comments
½ tsp	4 mins	Stir once.
½ tsp	6-7 mins	Rearrange after 4 minutes.
½ tsp	7-9 mins	Stir once.
½ tsp	5-6 mins	Stir two or three times.
½ tsp	7-9 mins	Rearrange after 4 minutes.
½ tsp	6-7 mins	Stir once.
½ tsp	8-10 mins	Stir once.
½ tsp	5-7 mins	Stir once.
—	5-7 mins	Stir once. Add salt after cooking.
—	8 mins	Arrange in a single layer.
—	10-12 mins	Dot with butter. Turn once.
½ tsp	5-7 mins	Stir once.
—	5-6 mins	Add salt after cooking
—	5-7 mins	Stir once. Add salt after cooking.
—	4-6 mins	Sprinkle salt over onions after cooking.
½ tsp	5-6 mins	
½ tsp	6-7 mins	
½ tsp	6-7 mins	

Type of Vegetable	Quantity	Water
Peppers, *diced*	175 g (6 oz)	4 tbsp (¼ cup)
Potatoes, New	250 g (½ lb)	4 tbsp (¼ cup)
Spinach, *leaf or chopped*	250 g (½ lb)	–

Reheating

Canned and fresh vegetables	Remove from can, put in dish three-quarters covered, cook on full power. Allow 1 minute per serving. Temperature should reach 70°C/160°F.
Mashed potatoes	As above but allow standing time.
Chips, (French fries)	Place in dish lined with absorbent kitchen paper towels; season to taste. Microwave on full until very hot.

Salt	Cooking Time	Comments
½ tsp	6-7 mins	
½ tsp	7-8 mins	Stir twice.
–	6-7 mins	Break up block 2 or 3 times. Add salt after cooking.
		Stir once during heating and once after.
		Stir once during cooking. Cooking time will depend on quantity of chips.

Acknowledgments

The publishers would like to acknowledge the following photographers: Bryce Attwell 59; Rex Bamber 43; Laurie Evans 7, 46; Robert Golden 83; Melvin Grey 2-3, 30, 35, 54-5; Gina Harris 63, 71, 74-5; Paul Kemp 51, 62; Peter Myers 11, 38-9, 78-9, 82; Roger Phillips 27, 66-7; and Charlie Stebbings 18.
Illustrations: Lily Whitlock.
The publishers would also like to thank Lakeland Plastics for their co-operation and the photographs on pages 15, 19 and 23.

Index